Jack,
Merry Christmas 2011!

OUR TIME – ANOTHER BOND

Eric

OUR TIME – ANOTHER BOND

ERIC HUGHES

Copyright © 2011 by Eric Hughes.

Library of Congress Control Number: 2010917900
ISBN: Hardcover   978-1-4568-2405-1
           Softcover   978-1-4568-2404-4
           Ebook   978-1-4568-2406-8

All rights reserved. No part of this book may be reproduced or transmitted in any form or by any means, electronic or mechanical, including photocopying, recording, or by any information storage and retrieval system, without permission in writing from the copyright owner.

This book was printed in the United States of America.

To order additional copies of this book, contact:
Xlibris Corporation
1-888-795-4274
www.Xlibris.com
Orders@Xlibris.com
90854

To my family and friends

I owe my inspiration for my story in part to the song by Jesse Belvin, "Goodnight My Love."

-Eric Hughes

Acknowledgements

My sincere thanks to Ms. Susan Mary Malone, Malone Editorial Services; and Ms. Rachel Cartwright, Literary Design, for their outstanding editorial service and guidance.

I also thank Ms. Linda Thornburg, Word Wizards Inc., for her sound editorial work.

My sincere gratitude to Fred Harper Illustrations, Inc., New York, N.Y. for the picturesque front cover; and to SABB Photography, Washington, D.C., for the professional back cover.

-Eric Hughes

Our Time – Another Bond, is a poignant story of an interracial romance during the early struggle for civil rights in the Sixties and of the relationship, rekindled thirty-five years later.

Chapter 1

Paul jogged slowly along the powder-white sands in the heat of Barbados, the quintessential coral British Island cradled in the multi-hued Caribbean Sea. He and his wife, Terri, were enjoying the soothing breezes and crystalline waters on their first vacation outside the United States together in several years.

As Paul neared a small bar on the beach, an old song wafted through the air. It reminded him of his high school days. He slowed down and stopped under the bar roof, safe from the hot sun. He ambled slowly in the direction of the music and, as he got closer, smiled and listened to the words:

> "Goodnight my love
> Pleasant dreams and sleep tight, my love
> May tomorrow be sunny and bright
> And bring you closer to me
>
> Before you go
> There's just one thing I'd like to know
> Is your love is still warm for me
> Or has it gone cold?

If you should awake in the still of the night
Please have no fear
For I'll be there, darling you know I care
Please give your love to me, dear, only

Goodnight my love
Pleasant dreams and sleep tight, my love
May tomorrow be sunny and bright
And bring you closer to me."

He sang along, oblivious to the lively crowd around him. He remembered the girl he fell in love with in high school, Irene Dudash.

"Damn, that was our song. Geez, I forgot all about it. Irene and I loved the hell out of that song."

"May I help you, sir?" asked the bartender.

Paul didn't answer.

"Sir, can I get you something from the bar?"

"Oh, I'm sorry. No thanks. I don't have my wallet with me."

Paul strolled back to where he left Terri under the beach umbrella. As he walked he was consumed with thoughts of Irene, their hot relationship as adolescents and young adults. He hadn't seen her in more than thirty years.

Terri asked, "Honey, where are we dining tonight?"

Paul picked up his towel without answering.

"Paul, are we eating tonight?"

"Yeah, I guess so."

"What do you mean, you guess so. What's wrong, you don't feel well?"

"I'm all right, but I'm not ready for dinner tonight. Maybe I can get you something from one of the road venders. I understand they have good grilled chicken, ribs, and fish. What do you want?"

Terri's mouth tightened. "Look, Paul, this is the last night of our vacation and you want to get me a carry-out from a street vender? I don't think so. Let's go to that cute little French restaurant by the pier we saw yesterday. That would put the icing on our vacation."

"Terri, I don't know what's gotten into me, but I don't want to go out tonight. Can we take a rain check on dinner?"

Terri's forehead wrinkled and she twisted her mouth as she picked up her towel and stomped toward the resort pool. Meanwhile, Paul walked slowly back to the hotel room.

He had never been overcome by thoughts of Irene before. While he had periodic flashbacks over the years, the song, "Goodnight My Love," stirred up something that he knew was not going away any time soon. It was their signature song and they danced to it many, many times.

Just thinking of Irene was not going to be the end of it. Not now!

"What should I do next? I must find Irene, see her, find out her marital status, maybe establish a platonic relationship with her. Is Irene alive? Does she want me to contact her, and how am I going to do all of this without telling Terri? Well, I'll just have to tell Terri and hope she understands. I must be crazy, jeopardizing my thirty-year marriage with this outrageous pursuit, but I've just got to do it!"

Paul walked to the window and stared at the orange sun as it disappeared into the Caribbean Sea. He sat on the bed and hummed the song that got him thinking of Irene again.

Chapter 2

Paul went to the post office and retrieved the large amount of mail stored during their vacation. He shuffled through it. One particular envelope, from his hometown, Becton, New York, caught his eye. The Becton High School Reunion Committee had sent an invitation to attend his thirty-fifth class reunion. He walked briskly into the house and sat down on the brown velour couch. As he absorbed the contents of the letter, he began to perspire. He took a deep breath and stared straight ahead at the beautiful, multi-colored Haitian painting on the wall.

He talked aloud, something he was prone to do when stressed out.

"I wonder if Oscar, Tim, and Arvin are planning to attend. Man, I haven't seen those guys in thirty years. And damn, what a coincidence. I was just thinking about Irene – what timing! I wonder if she'll attend. Whew! We had a turbulent relationship in high school that nearly caused riots and divided the school and community along racial lines."

Paul rose from the couch and strolled to the window. "Our relationship was risky and dangerous, almost unheard of back then. It's hard to believe that I haven't seen her in more than thirty years."

The blood in his heart pumped rapidly. He wanted to see Irene again and needed to know if she planned to attend. She had missed the past four reunions. "I've got to find out for sure if she'll be there."

Paul thought about the reunion for hours. Suddenly, he ran to the attic, taking two stairs at a time, and pulled out a large box containing items from his past. His high school yearbook was near the bottom. He eased it out gently, brushed it off, and opened the faded book to page sixty-six. Paul stared at the photo of Irene Dudash for several minutes and smiled slowly, nodding.

He returned to the living room, yearbook in hand, sat on the couch, and stared at the phone.

Finally, he picked it up, dialed information, and received the telephone number of the Becton High School Reunion Committee chairperson.

"Hello, this is Betty Turner-Burns. May I help you?"

"Mrs. Burns, my name is Paul Hodge, class of 1968. Is Turner your maiden name?"

"Yes, Paul. We took chemistry and biology together."

"That was so long ago, Betty. How are you? Long time no see."

"Just fine. What can I do for you, Paul?"

"Can you tell me whether Irene Dudash has confirmed attendance at the upcoming reunion?"

"Just a minute. Yes, she confirmed yesterday. Incidentally, her present name is Irene Dudash-Covington."

"Thanks so much, Betty. I hope to see you in a few months."

Paul slowly hung up the phone. It wasn't good enough for him that Irene confirmed attendance at the reunion – Paul had to hear it from Irene. "But how am I going to get in touch with her?" Paul mumbled to himself. The Internet!

* * *

Paul sat down at the computer and searched for contact information for Irene Dudash-Covington. He entered her full name in: the State of New York. No matches! Then he repeated her name nationwide. A match! A name and telephone number in Chicago, Illinois.

He picked up the phone and nervously dialed 312 661-4571. It rang once. Paul abruptly hung up the phone. He thought a few minutes – then dialed the number again and let it ring.

A soft voice said, "Hello."

"Hello, I'm looking for Ms. Covington, Ms. Dudash-Covington. Is this her number?"

"Who is calling, please?"

"My name is Paul Hodge," Paul said nervously. "We went to high school together I'm trying to reach her."

A deadening silence!

"Hello, Hello. Are you there?" Paul asked.

Finally the voice at the other end said, "This is Irene, Paul. It's good to hear your voice. How have you been?"

"I've been very good. How about you?"

"I've been very well, thank you. And to what do I owe this very surprising phone call?"

"Are you planning to attend the upcoming reunion? I'm kind of undecided, but if you're planning to be there, I'll certainly attend. We have about thirty years of conversation to make up."

"Well, I thought it was about time that I attended our class reunion. I missed the last four, so, yes, I plan on attending. Other classmates have encouraged me to go. It will be good to see everyone again."

"Good, what do you – ?"

"Paul, are you married and do you have children?"

"Yes, I'm married and we have one daughter. I live in Washington, D.C., where I had a great career with Bartlett Foods. I'm retired now. What about you?"

"I'm a widow and my daughter passed away last year from cancer. I'm a school superintendent in Chicago and enjoy my work. Otherwise, I live a very normal life and except for the cold weather, I love the Chicago area."

"Oh, I'm very sorry to hear about your losses. I can't imagine what you've been through."

"Well, each day I've learned to adjust to life and, yes, it is a difficult transition."

"I remember you as a strong person with a will to overcome adversity. It appears that you haven't changed."

"I don't think I have, either. I'm going out to dinner with my girlfriend so I must cut our conversation short. I'm glad you took the initiative to call me and I look forward to seeing you at the reunion."

"Great, see you then. Wait a minute, wait a minute, don't hang up."

"What is it, Paul?"

"I have a question to ask you. When was the last time you heard the song, 'Goodnight My Love?'"

Silence!

Suddenly, Irene responded, "Paul, I haven't heard it in years but I remember it very well. We had some good times listening to that song. Wow! I do remember it."

"And guess where I heard the song recently?"

"I have no idea."

"I went on a Caribbean vacation recently and as I jogged on the beach, I heard the song playing on the radio at a beach bar. I stopped abruptly, listened to the entire song, and immediately thought about you. Now I know why people say that music is very important in their everyday lives. It revives and stimulates memories."

"Wow! That is very interesting, Paul. Okay, we can discuss this in full at the reunion but I've really got to run now. I hope to see you soon."

"Bye, Irene."

Paul screamed after hanging up the phone. He smiled as he pumped his fist and arm up and down several times.

* * *

Irene ran her bath water, sprinkled in some bubble bath and walked slowly to the bedroom. She picked up a box of hair curlers and sat down, then jumped up and ran back to the bathroom to turn off the faucet.

"I wonder why Paul called me," Irene thought out loud. "Does he still have feelings for me or was he just being nice? Wow! I never got over him. Has he changed over the years? Is he still romantic? Will I look good to him? But he said he's married, so what the hell am I getting so hot about? Okay! Okay! I've got to stop this torture."

Irene curled her hair, wrapped it, and slowly eased into the hot tub. She scooted down up to her neck. "Ooh, this feels sooo good." The warm, scented bubble water stimulated Irene and evoked more thoughts about Paul.

"Wow, Paul was the man back then – and he was *my* man – tall, athletic, handsome, base voice, and perfect posture. I wonder how he looks. I'm sure glad I've been exercising over the years because I don't look bad for a dame of fifty-two, do I?" Irene grabbed a face cloth and splashed the now lukewarm water on her face and shoulders. She exited the tub, toweled herself off, and sat on the bed, staring down at the floor.

Irene put on her pink silk robe and dialed her close friend.

"Hi, Claire. You busy?"

"I'm just finishing up some paperwork for tomorrow. How'd your day go?"

"It was fantastic, just fantastic!"

"Okay, I've never heard you sound so excited. What's up?"

"You'll never guess what happened to me today. I received a call today from a guy named Paul. I grew up with him and we dated in high school. He was a good-looking black guy. I haven't seen him in over thirty years and he calls and asks if I'm going to our class reunion. Can you believe that?"

"Well, are you going?"

"Are you kidding? Hell, yes, I'm going! Especially now that I know he'll be there." Irene laughed loudly as she breathed heavily into the telephone.

"It sounds like you still got the hots for this guy. Just be careful. Did you check out his status – I mean, is he married, has a girlfriend, or . . ."

"He's married, but I didn't get into other particulars. Hell, I'm just happy that he called. I'll find out all the other information when I see him. Claire, I'm nervous as hell. Please kick me if I order dessert when we dine tonight – I can't afford to put on any weight. I've got to look good for Paul. Ha, Ha, Ha."

"Now, Irene, I can feel your excitement and expectations, but my advice is to go into this thing slowly and don't expect matters to be like they were thirty years ago. I just don't want you to get hurt or get yourself into trouble. Truthfully, you sound very vulnerable."

Silence.

"You know, I'm fifty-two years of age and I guess I never knew that middle-aged people could be as stimulated and excited as I am today. It's a great feeling! I feel like a kid going to her first prom. I haven't had anything this exciting happen to me in quite a few years so I'm sort of letting it have its way with me. I feel good! And guess what? I am not apologizing for how I feel because it's very natural."

"Okay, okay, don't get so defensive about it. I've got to meet Paul. In all the years I've known you, I don't know of anyone else who appears to have made a little girl of you again. You haven't even seen him yet and you've been swept off of your feet already. What's next?"

"Well, I don't know." Irene walked to the calendar and circled the date of the reunion. "This excitement might die down, but, wow, I love the feeling. What should I wear to the reunion?"

"Something dashing, elegant, eye-catching, powerful, and, definitely, sexy. Don't forget to show plenty of cleavage – it works every time. Ha, Ha, Ha." Claire laughed so loud that Irene had to pull the telephone receiver away from her ear for a second.

"Okay, don't get carried away. I get your drift. In other words, you never get a second chance to make a good first impression."

"You got it, kiddo!" Claire said.

* * *

"Honey, how was work today?" Paul asked Terri.

"Great. Macy's regional manager informed me today that I've been reassigned to the position of retail merchandise manager of Liz Claiborne ladies' and Polo men's departments in our local store. We have to purchase new seasonal stock and get ready for our annual trade shows and seminars.

"Does that mean you've been promoted?"

"Oh, yeah!" Terri said nodding her head.

"That's great," Paul said as he walked over and kissed Terri on the cheek.

Terri removed her black high heels and headed to the kitchen for a glass of water.

"I'd like to discuss something with you," Paul said.

"Okay, I want to change into something more comfortable. I'll be right back."

Terri headed to the bedroom, humming the old popular musical standard, "Lullaby of Birdland," and returned within minutes to the living room where Paul was sitting on the couch. She gently sat down beside him, turned sideways, and placed both legs across his lap.

"Okay, what's up?"

Paul shifted positions and avoided eye contact. He wrung his sweaty hands nervously and placed them on her legs. He cleared his throat several times and raised his head. Their eyes finally met.

"Well, I just received notice of my thirty-fifth high school class reunion, which I'm planning to attend. It's going to be great seeing my old friends again."

"I'm glad you're planning to attend because I know how important it is to you to renew past friendships. You're very good about things like that and keeping in touch with the past. I wish I had your drive to do the same."

"I have something to share with you." Paul took a deep breath and let the air out.

Frown lines appeared on Terri's forehead. "Paul, you're scaring me. What's wrong?"

"I dated a white girl in high school and our relationship caused an uproar. Our parents, the teachers, our friends, and other nosy people tried to break it up, but we continued our affair. We were so into each other. Anyway, Irene probably will be at the reunion.

"And?"

"Well, I haven't seen her in over thirty years and I want to keep in touch with her, even after the reunion. But I just wanted you to know because it's been on my mind.

We're just friends now. That's it. I'm telling you now because I don't want to keep anything from you."

Terri's jaw dropped. She slowly removed her long legs from his lap and sat straight up on the edge of the couch. "Paul, what are you trying to say? Do you want to see your former white lover now that you're an older adult, to get back with her because society wouldn't approve of it in the 1960's? Is that what you mean?"

"No." The palms of his hands flew open, appealing for Terri to be reasonable. "You don't understand."

"You're damned right I don't understand and I'm still waiting for an explanation."

"Terri, all I want to do is to see her at the reunion and renew a friendship. That's it! I'm not interested in having an affair. You already know how I like to revisit the past – that's who I am. Remember the time when I went to Alabama to find Billy Bradshaw? How about the time I went to California to locate Jesse Reyes?"

"Paul. You just mentioned two males. No females. Wouldn't you say that this is just a little different?"

"This may sound different, but it's my honest intention," Paul responded.

"I don't quite understand what the hell this is all about. I want you to see your old friends, but the way you presented this situation about this white lady is weird. Why didn't you tell me about her before?"

"There was no need to. You never asked about my adolescent relationships and I never said anything about it. We were in high school. We were just babies."

"But honestly, Paul, can't you see how this is different? I don't want to belabor the point, but suppose the situation were reversed and I wanted to go to a high school reunion, specifically to seek out a former male classmate, who happened to be white. What would be your reaction?"

Paul nodded. He bowed his head for a second and quickly raised it before speaking. "Yes, I can see your concerns, but please trust me on this, Terri. I have nothing to hide. And please don't interject race into this discussion. If Irene were purple, I'd still want to maintain a friendly relationship with her."

"Look, I'm not interjecting race here, but you're not going to tell a 'sister' how white women operate.

"They're aggressive, they take no prisoners, and will do anything to get in bed with whomever they pursue, especially black men. You know, we sisters have a long institutional memory about how white women have won over our black men by spoiling and giving them anything they ask for. But go ahead, Paul. You have a good time at the reunion."

"Do you think I'd risk losing . . . ?"

"Okay, I don't want to talk about this anymore." Terri rose abruptly and headed to the bedroom. She slammed the door behind her.

"What did I stir up?" Paul said, scratching his head.

CHAPTER 3

The excitement of attending the reunion and possibly seeing Irene again was too much to keep inside. Paul called one of his best high school buddies to share his good feelings.

"Hey, Oscar, this is Paul Hodge."

"You mean the Paul Hodge who almost started riots in high school by dating a white girl named Irene Dudash?"

"Hey, man, give me a break. I was just doing my thing."

"Yeah, we can laugh about it now but you and Irene almost divided the Becton community along racial lines. Ha, ha, man, those were some shaky times."

"I know. Are you going to our thirty-fifth reunion?"

"Hell, yes. I haven't been to one in thirty years."

"I'm going, too, and guess who's planning to attend?"

"Please Paul, don't say Irene Dudash."

"Bingo!"

"Have you been in touch with her all these years?"

"No, but I damn sure want to see her. She's already confirmed her attendance."

"What was it that drew both of you together? I do remember her as being a cool white girl, hipper than other white girls, and some black ones, too. I agree that she had it going on."

"Yeah, and I soaked it all up."

"It doesn't sound like you ever got over her, Paul."

"Oh, she came across my mind many, many times in the past thirty years. You know, I told Terri about Irene and she didn't take it too well."

"You did *what*? Well, what did you expect?"

"I told Terri that Irene and I had dated in high school and that she probably would be at the reunion. I didn't tell her that I also dated her when I left the military. I told Terri that I wanted to have a platonic relationship with Irene."

"Man that was a bold move. I wouldn't have told Kitty because I know she'd hit the ceiling."

"Life is too short, Oscar. I'm retired now and Terri knows that I'm about re-establishing friendships. She's a little upset now, but she'll be all right."

* * *

Paul pushed ahead with his reunion agenda. He wanted to look his best. Appearance and neatness had always been important to him. He drove four hours to New York's garment district to shop for his special outfit, finally deciding on a smart black Jhane Barnes three-button pinstripe suit with a four-button double-breasted vest. He bought a box of one-hundred-percent cotton white handkerchiefs to place one in his front top pocket, with four peaks showing above. He added a pure white Geoffrey Bean one-hundred-percent cotton dress shirt with a British spread collar and French cuffs, and picked out a silk burgundy tie to bring out the suit. At Macy's, Paul found a pair of black Johnston & Murphy wing tip dress shoes, perfect for the occasion. Finally, he stopped at Burberry's and purchased a three-ounce bottle of sharp, spicy, lavender and amber fragrance Burberry cologne.

Back home he pulled out his high school yearbook again. He studied it to refresh his mind about Irene's school activities. "I want to impress her with my memories after all these years. Okay, I remember that she was one of the best cheerleaders in school, her bubbly personality and charm stood out, both of us were good conversationalists, which was one of the things that connected us, and we participated in many school activities together."

Paul smiled. Almost instantly, he frowned with memories of the trying times. "Those white students couldn't stand seeing us together and it's a wonder we weren't harmed. We sure got no support from the teachers, who didn't like it at all. And gee, my black friends didn't like our relationship either, especially the black females. It was a big sacrifice because I lost many friendships. But, hell, I was in love, I think, and I was just doing my thing. I hope they're not still carrying that negative baggage with them."

CHAPTER 4

The year 1967 witnessed increased opposition to the Vietnam War.

Domestically, racial riots broke out in Detroit because of police abuse, lack of affordable housing, economic inequality, urban renewal projects, black militancy, and other reasons. In sports, the Green Bay Packers and the Kansas City Chiefs played in the first Super Bowl. Thurgood Marshall made legal and racial history by becoming the first African-American judge to serve on the U.S. Supreme Court.

Paul Hodge attended Becton High School, located in New York State, approximately sixty miles northwest of New York City. Most of the students came from working-class families. Becton was known for employing many local factory workers. The major products were fiberglass, copper, iron, oil, gasoline, and glass.

Becton's population was 13,000, of which eighty-eight percent were white, six-percent African-American, three-percent Hispanic, two-percent Asian-American, and one percent, other races.

At Becton High School, a petite sixteen-year old white girl, sharply dressed in a short brown tweed, pleated skirt and yellow cashmere short-sleeved sweater, penny loafers, and with coal black hair sat down at a desk directly across from Paul. It happened to be the first day of their junior year in high school. Paul wore a light blue button-collared shirt, charcoal gray slacks, a red vest with gold buttons, and burgundy Bass Weejun loafers.

The girl turned toward Paul, her blue eyes sparkling, and with a big grin showing her almost perfectly lined white teeth, and said, "Hi, my name is Irene."

Paul responded, "Hi, my name is Paul." They both smiled and sat quietly for a brief moment, looking around the room at the other students.

"Do you know anyone in this class?" Irene asked

"No. Do you?"

"No. What class do you have next period?

Paul checked his schedule. "I have geometry in Room 830. I believe the teacher's name is Ms. Putnam. Where are you next period?

"I have French III with Ms. Gilchrist."

The bell rang, and Irene and Paul said goodbye and headed to their next classes. They continued their friendship the next several weeks, often walking down the hallways together at Becton High School. They were noticed. Stern stares from white students and curious looks from black students occurred whenever Irene and Paul were seen together. Even the teachers couldn't stop their periodic glances, in apparent disgust.

One day after school, Irene ran and caught up with Paul as he exited the boy's gymnasium.

"Paul, are you going to the pep rally this afternoon?"

"I may. Everyone will be there."

"Let's go together."

Paul was astonished. He said nothing at first, but after having had time to absorb what Irene said, responded, "Well, I don't know, Irene. You know there'll be bulging eyes and wagging tongues if we go together."

"What do you mean?" Irene asked, with the whites of her eyes expanded and mouth wide open.

"Look, your white friends are not going to dig it if we appear together. My black friends, especially the girls, will freak out. That's not very hip."

"So what? Irene responded as she stared at him, her mouth twisted with anger and her hands on her hips. "I don't care. I want to go with you."

"Well, I want to go with you, too, but people will be looking and talking about us."

Irene inhaled, then exhaled slowly and rolled her eyes toward the sky in disgust. "Don't sweat it. They're going to talk anyway, let's face it. I'm a very independent-thinking person and being with you in public doesn't bother me. That's *their* problem."

"Would your parents approve of us socializing? You mean to tell me they wouldn't be upset with you? C'mon, Irene. Honestly."

"Hell, I don't care. I get excellent grades in school, I complete my chores, and I work summers so my parents won't have to give me an allowance." Then she calmed down enough to respond to Paul's question. "No, they probably wouldn't like it at all. But it's not like I'm asking you to come to my house for dinner, although I would like to."

"You're getting too upset about this conversation. Let's change the subject."

"What's the matter, no stomach for facing the truth?" Irene asked with a sarcastic smile. Her slowly changing demeanor soothed Paul for the apparent standoff they were headed for.

"Yeah, I can take it," Paul said with a smile.

* * *

"Paul, did you hear about those beatings of Freedom marchers yesterday in Selma, Alabama?" Irene asked.

Paul nodded. "It was all over the news. Man, I wouldn't want to live down there with all that racism going on."

"Well, it's here, too. There are white people here with those same feelings that keep them hidden. They can act the same way."

That scenario scared Paul. "Yeah, I guess you're right."

Paul could not deny that he had a flutter in his heart for Irene. She turned him on with her looks, her tasteful clothes, aggressive manner and, above all, she was hip. He wanted to be with her, too.

* * *

"Dad, can I borrow the car? I'm going to the library."

"Sure, son. The keys are on my dresser," Mr. Hodge responded.

Paul picked up Irene and headed to a secluded place near the outskirts of town and parked.

The near full moon brightened the night. The warm breeze and the scent of honeysuckle sweetened the air. Paul turned the radio dial to WNJR, a rhythm and blues station out of Newark, New Jersey, with a largely black listening audience.

"Is it all right to leave the radio on this station or would you rather listen to something else?" Paul asked.

"No, leave it on that station. I love this music. What's your favorite group, Paul?"

"Oh, the Temptations and the Four Tops are bad, and the Impressions, Archie Bell and the Drells, Delfonics, and the Intruders are also great. I also like some of the older groups like the Penguins, Moonglows, and Spaniels, groups you probably never heard of. Do you have any favorites?"

"I like Shep & the Limelites, Isley Brothers, Flamingos, Clovers, Chantels, Channels, Five Satins, Hank Ballard & the Midnighters, Little Anthony & the Imperials, and the Paragons, who later changed their name to the Jesters."

Paul looked at Irene with his mouth opened wide enough to catch flies. He said nothing for several seconds. "Irene, how did you . . .

"My favorite songs are 'Personality' by Lloyd Price, 'Earth Angel' by the Penguins, 'A Thousand Miles Away' by the Heartbeats, 'A Little Bit of Soap' by the Jarmels, and my all-time favorite, 'I Need Your Lovin Every Day,' by Don Gardner."

A startled Paul almost crossed the double lines in the street, closely avoiding a head-on collision with an oncoming car.

"How in the hell did you know about these songs and artists?"

"One day I was flipping through the radio stations and came across WNJR. I didn't realize that it was a black station until I started paying attention to the lyrics and the different emphasis the singers placed on the words. I had never heard that before. It was a gas! So I realized long ago that black people are very talented and creative but aren't given credit for their artistry. I listen to the station every night in my room with the volume turned down so my parents and sister can't hear."

"You are so cool," Paul said, laughing loudly. "And just think, I thought you knew nothing of this type of music. Man, this is a lesson to me. I'll never prejudge anyone again."

Paul and Irene exited the car and leaned side-by-side against the fender as the disk jockey played, "Oh, What A Night," by the Dells. They looked at each other with nothing said.

Then Irene broke the silence. "Where is our relationship going?"

"What do you mean?"

"Where is this relationship going, what do we want from each other?"

"I don't know." He waited for Irene to make her move, but he didn't have all night. He had to get Irene and the car back home. He kissed her lips. Irene responded by putting her arms around Paul and held on tightly, pressing her body to his. Paul immediately was aroused. Irene pressed harder and harder and they were in full embrace.

"Oh, Paul, I want you so much."

"I want you, too, but we've got to be careful."

"I know, but how long are we going to let this feeling go on?"

"Okay, let's split," Paul said without responding to Irene's question. My father will be looking for me and I want to get the car again."

"Have you settled down yet?" Irene asked as she smiled sheepishly.

"Barely," Paul responded with a smile.

As they headed home, the radio played "Goodnight My Love." They squeezed each other's hands, tightly.

*   *   *

"Hey, guess what?"

"You're ready to have sex with me?" Irene responded.

"No. I mean, yes. No, look, I just received my track varsity jacket and letter. That was one of the goals I set for myself last year."

"Oh, I'm so proud of you. I can't wait to wear it."

"*Wear* it?" Paul asked.

"Yes, wear it. Don't you know that it's customary for a girlfriend to wear her boyfriend's varsity jacket? It means they're going together."

"Well, I don't know."

"What do you mean, 'You don't know'?"

"That's going to start some mess in school."

"Well, that's too bad. Wow, I'm proud of you, Paul."

Chapter 5

The next day Paul and Oscar stood by a park bench near the school, exchanging small talk when Irene appeared.

"Hi, Paul. How ya doing?"

"Hi. I'm doing okay. Irene, this is Oscar. Oscar, this is Irene." They exchanged handshakes.

"Oscar, can you excuse us for a minute?" Paul asked.

"Yeah, man, go ahead."

Irene grabbed Paul by the arm and walked about twenty yards away from Oscar.

"Can I wear your jacket to school?"

"I don't know if I'm ready for this. I just got it yesterday. What's the hurry?"

"There's no hurry, I just want to wear it now."

Paul slowly removed his jacket and helped Irene drape it over her shoulders.

"Hey, Oscar, we're going to class. I'll see you later."

"Okay, man, later."

Paul and Irene began walking together toward the school entrance. Irene ignored the looks and stares they received from the white students that gathered near the school entrance, but they made Paul nervous. Black students also appeared confused.

As they entered the school, a voice shouted out, "Get that N-word's jacket off your back, you N-word lover."

Paul whipped his head in the direction of the comment. Shortly thereafter someone else screamed, "Why don't you stick with your own kind? We can find a rope and tree here, just like they use down in Mississippi and Alabama." Several laughs came from the white students in response to the comment.

"Yeah, but you forgot one thing," Paul yelled out to no one in particular. "We ain't going to take that shit like the blacks in the South. So come on with it."

Irene pulled Paul away from the crowd and quickly led him inside the building to the basement stairs. Before she could open her mouth, a shaken Paul said, "See, this is what I meant. I like you a lot but it ain't cool hanging around you at school."

"Okay, okay. Don't sweat it, we'll work out something. Wow, that was a raunchy scene. I told you there are racists in this school. Look, try to forget what happened here and I'll see you later," Irene said, handing Paul his jacket.

As Paul proceeded to his first class, Mr. Bell, a white social studies teacher approached him from behind. "Hello, son. What's your name?"

Paul turned around and stopped. "My name is Paul Hodge."

"My name is Mr. Bell."

"Well, Paul, I witnessed that ugly scene a few minutes ago and it was a very unfortunate incident. I don't know what your relationship is with that girl, but you better try to tone it down. We have good race relations in this school and in this community. I wouldn't want to see that change."

"So what are you trying to say?"

"You know what I mean. Be smart, son, and hang out with your own kind."

"First of all, I'm not your damn son. Furthermore, you ain't got nothin to do with this. I should tell the principal that you're harassing me and making racist statements. Yeah, that's what I should do."

"Now wait a minute, young fella, I was just advising you for your own good."

"Yeah, you go off when you see a white girl and black guy digging each other, don't you? Well, get used to it."

As Paul walked quickly past Mr. Bell, Mr. Bell stood there, gently rubbing his chin.

* * *

"Hey, Oscar, man, I gotta rap to you after class. You wouldn't believe what happened this morning."

"Okay. I'm leaving as soon as I run some sprints and do my pushups. The teacher is gone for the day."

Paul and Oscar exited the gymnasium and headed toward the football field for privacy. Paul walked quickly and Oscar followed closely behind at the same pace. They sat in the bleacher seats.

"Man, I walked with Irene past a group of whites and they called me all kinds of racist names. They went off when they saw Irene wearing my varsity jacket. I hollered back at them. Then this teacher named Mr. Bell came up to me and suggested that I cool it with Irene and not cause a scene. Can you believe that shit? Man, I was ticked off."

"What did you do?"

"Nothing. I just told him I was going to report him to the principal for what he said to me. He backed off a little. You know what? This whole Irene scene is going to get worse because I'm beginning to have feelings for her. She's a choice chick."

"I'm hip with that, man, but there will be some heavy pressure on you. Her parents will find out and all hell is going to break loose. And what about your parents? They're bound to find out. The black chicks are going to give you hell, so be ready for them. Have you thought about how you're going to handle all this?"

"Damn, Oscar, whose side are you on? I thought you were my man. I need your help; I don't need all these questions." Paul immediately grabbed his head with both hands. He shook his head from side to side.

Silence!

"I'm sorry, man. I didn't mean to snap at you like that. Damn, man, what am I going to do?"

"You'll figure it out. You're strong-willed and I've always admired you for that part of your personality. Man, we've got to start acting like men. So, my brother, my advice is to follow your heart and let the chips fall where they may."

Paul looked at Oscar with admiration and smiled broadly. His chest stuck out with pride as a result of his conversation with Oscar. Both boys stepped down from the bleachers with their arms around each other's shoulders.

CHAPTER 6

Paul usually spent summers around Becton, hanging out with friends and doing odd jobs to earn spending money. However, he would spend the summer of 1967 in a completely different environment.

Paul's cousin, Quentin, attended Shaw University in Raleigh, North Carolina and wanted Paul to get the feel for college life. Quentin also wanted to expose and educate Paul about a new black movement in the U.S. The new organization was named the Student Nonviolent Coordinating Committee, or SNCC.

"Hey, cuz, you're a mature kid. I know you're a little young to fully understand this, but try hard because it may affect your life as you get older. Okay?" Quentin asked.

"Yeah, go ahead. I'm listening," Paul said as he leaned over the table.

"We black people are under assault by white oppression. We have no real freedom, we can't eat where we want, we're being murdered when we try to exercise our rights, we have piss-poor jobs, and our kids have no future. SNCC was formed to fight these oppressions by organizing sit-ins and demanding equality."

"What's happening this summer?" Paul asked.

"There will be a bunch of sit-ins. I want you to visit Shaw and experience them. You might want to think about attending Shaw. It's a good school, and they have plenty of good looking chicks."

Paul smiled and said, "Let's go."

* * *

Paul traveled to Raleigh and SNCC headquarters where he got a chance to meet SNCC leaders, John Lewis, Julian Bond, and others. He absorbed all he could about "the struggle."

Paul witnessed beatings of unarmed peaceful protesters, water-hosed protesters, and many bloodied by police billy clubs. But he also saw an organization destined to trudge into new territory by protesting the war in Vietnam, and challenging the government about bringing to justice the senseless murders of black people.

He returned to Becton more knowledgeable than any of his peers about what it meant as a black person to fight for freedom in America.

He shared his experience with his best friend, Oscar.

"Man, you should have been there. These new jokers in SNCC ain't taking any more shit from white people. They're supposed to practice nonviolence, but I saw some guys carrying guns and other weapons."

"Are you joining SNCC when you go to college?" Oscar asked.

"Probably will. I might even attend Shaw. I'll really be close to the action then."

"How you gonna act when you return to Becton? We don't have many blacks, and fewer blacks in high school. Do you think you'll be hostile towards whites?" Oscar asked.

"No. As long as they don't mess with me. No doubt, Oscar, I have a new outlook on white America and how we blacks are getting shafted."

* * *

Paul looked forward to his final year at Becton High School. He wanted to improve on his good grades and prepare for college.

On this particular day, on April 4, 1968, he had homework to do, but he chose first to watch *Mission Impossible*. He lay back on his bed and the thoughts of his conversation with Oscar remained on his mind. A news bulletin came across the screen:

"Dr. Martin Luther King, Jr. was assassinated today in Memphis, Tennessee."

Paul jumped up from the bed in total disbelief.

He ran out of his room, crying uncontrollably, and screaming for his parents. "Mom, Dad, where are you? They killed Dr. King in Memphis. Can you believe it? Why did they have to kill him? Oh, they really messed up now."

Paul's parents sat on the living room couch watching the horrible news and clinging to each other. Tears streamed down their cheeks as Paul sat down next to them.

"We're not going to take this," Paul's mother said in a halting, nervous voice. "There's going to be hell to pay."

"I thought we were making progress but this will set us back for sure," Mr. Hodge said.

Many thoughts ran through Paul's head. Who did it? Who is going to lead our people? Will there be riots? How will this impact on his relationship with Irene?

* * *

Paul ran to the phone and called Oscar. "Man, did you hear about King?

"No, what happened?"

"Those white bastards killed him in Memphis."

"Are you serious?"

"No shit man, they killed him dead on a hotel balcony. He's dead, Oscar, dead, man."

"The shit's really going to hit the fan now. I'm going to watch the news and I'll call you later," Oscar said.

* * *

Paul placed his finger on the receiver, released it, and dialed Irene's number. Busy. He tried again and again but it was tied up. He called the operator.

"I have an emergency call for 212 554-1234. The line has been busy for thirty-minutes now. My wife's having a baby and I need to contact her mother."

"Okay, sir, just a second." After a brief pause, the operator said, "Go ahead, sir, your party is on the line."

"Irene, did you hear the news?" Paul asked.

"Yes, I did. This is terrible," Irene said. "Wait a minute Paul – they just announced that a white man was seen running from the building next to where King was standing."

"Did they get the bastard?" Paul asked.

"Hold up, Paul – no, he got away. Well, black people will respond to this incident and it's not going to be pretty."

"Yeah, and I'm in a rumbling mood so no white person better not say anything to me." Paul's voice dripped with anger and hate.

"I know how you feel . . ."

"No! You don't know how I feel. You're not black so how can you possibly know how I *feel*?"

"Okay, I used a poor choice of words. I want to go crazy, too, but what good will it do? I'm going to watch more of the news, so let's talk later. Are you okay now?"

"I'll be all right. Later."

As the news of King's death exploded onto TV screens and radios across the country, pockets of boiling points in black neighborhoods ignited. The black neighborhoods of Atlanta, Newark, Washington, D.C., Memphis, Detroit, Chicago, Baltimore, and Los Angeles rioted, burning business establishments, breaking store windows, looting, overturning cars, and assaulting any white person within reach. It was one of the ugliest domestic incidents in American history. It was a reminder of one of Dr. King's famous, prophetic speeches as he assessed the future of race relations in America . . . ."Either we learn to live together as brothers and sisters or perish together as fools."

Chapter 7

Two months passed: Dr. King's death still bothered Paul. One Saturday he woke up early, dressed in his walking attire, and strolled through a park near his home. He wanted to be in a tranquil environment. The park, with its squirrels, birds, beautiful trees and flowers, and manicured grass provided that atmosphere. Paul's developing feelings for Irene stayed on his mind, given that the assassination of Dr. King worsened race relations in America. He feared that the escalation of his affair might harm peaceful race relations at the high school and in Becton. He didn't want to be perceived as sticking the relationship in the faces of whites or using Irene to get back at whites. Equally important, how would he be perceived by his black peers? Would he be ostracized? Would they despise him? Paul shouted, "Damn it, Irene's my girlfriend and we're not going to hide the relationship from anyone again."

Paul hurried home and called Irene. "Hi, are you busy?" Paul asked.

"Oh, I'm listening to this new song by O.C. Smith, "Little Green Apples." I think it's going to be a hit."

"Yeah, yeah, okay. Look, we need to talk in person. It's important." What is it?"

"Look, not over the phone, in person."

"But . . . ."

"Just do as I say and meet me at the corner of Silver Road and Miles Court in an hour."

"Okay."

* * *

Paul ran a few errands for his mother and then headed straight to the meeting spot. Irene arrived shortly after him, walking briskly as if someone was following her.

"What is it?" Irene asked. Paul said nothing immediately. A sneaky grin developed on his face. He reached gently for her hands, stared into her eyes, and asked, "Do you want to go steady with me?"

Silence!

The expression on her face changed to a grin, which became wider and wider. Her eyes started tearing. "Oh Paul, are you serious?"

"Yes, I am."

"Yes!" Irene said as she leaped into his arms.

Just as they completed their embrace, a group of white kids drove by, shouting racial epithets at them.

Paul said, "Well, get used to it, baby, because every time we're seen together, that's what we can expect."

"We'll make it because we really like each other. We'll do just fine."

"Yeah, but we haven't yet faced my black brothers and sisters. They're going to be brutal. The Dr. King assassination won't help matters. We've got to tell our parents because they're going to find out."

"I'm going to tell mine tonight. My father is not going to like it." Irene said.

"Yeah, and mine are not going to like it one bit, especially my mother," Paul responded.

* * *

"Irene, do you want to go to the movies?" Paul asked.

"Yes. What are we going to see?"

"Look, there is this movie about a white girl who brings her black boyfriend home to meet her parents, over dinner. Almost sounds like us. The name of it is *Guess Who's Coming to Dinner*, starring Katherine Hepburn, Spencer Tracy and Sidney Poitier. Maybe we can learn something. How about it?"

"Solid," Irene said, smiling broadly.

"But first I have to tell my parents about you. I'll call you later" Paul said.

* * *

Paul's mother had just called him and his dad for dinner, so the scene was set. "Paul, I have your favorite dinner tonight, so enjoy it." She placed on his plate two smothered pork chops, yellow squash mixed with onions, and candied yams.

"Thanks, Mom," Paul said.

"When am I going to get *my* choice of dinner?" Paul's father asked.

Paul's mother turned, winked at Paul, and smiled.

"Mom and Dad, I am dating a white girl in school and I want you to know before you hear it from someone else. I like her a lot, she's fine, and she's a lot of fun to be with."

Paul's parents looked at him as though he had lost his mind. "Son, you've got to be careful about this. These white folk in Becton aren't going to like it. Many of them think like those crackers in the South. I don't like it one bit. Let that girl go now before it's too late," Paul's father said.

Paul's mother shook her head and stared angrily at Paul. "Son, there's plenty of pretty black girls in the neighborhood. Why are you chasing those fast white girls?"

"I didn't chase her, in fact, I resisted her but she grew on me."

His mother added, "But Paul, these are some difficult times for race relations and you're putting yourself right smack in the middle of it."

"I know Mom, but I've made up my mind on this."

Paul nibbled at his food but wasn't in the mood for eating even his choice dinner. He excused himself from the table and went to his room.

* * *

"I told my parents about us. Like I thought, my parents have problems with it. Have you told your parents yet?" Paul asked.

"Yes, and it didn't go over well. My father went ape. He wants me to cut off our relationship."

"Well, it sounds like you're in deep trouble with your parents, too. What are you going do?" Paul asked.

"Keep seeing you, that's what. I'm the All-American girl, yet I'm still catching hell because I chose you as my boyfriend. You know, I think my parents are racists."

"You may be right and mine may be, too. Our relationship is the real test and they're not handling it well."

CHAPTER 8

The next day news came over the wires that track and field stars Tommy Smith and John Carlos displayed the Black Power salute at the 1968 Summer Olympic Games in Mexico City. They were expelled from the Olympic village for their actions. Whites said the act was a sign of disloyalty to America; blacks believed their actions were timely.

That evening, Paul and Irene went to the movies on their first public date. Irene held Paul's arm as they approached the ticket booth. After Paul purchased two tickets, they stood outside watching the other moviegoers. Two white couples with disgusted looks on their faces stared at Paul and Irene.

Irene recognized one of the white males, Tim, who said, "What's the matter, Irene, can't find a white boyfriend?"

Paul stepped toward the boy and said, "Hey, man, you trying to start something?"

"Nobody was talking to you, boy."

"If you want to jump bad, man, make your move." Paul took another step. Irene grabbed Paul by the arm and led him away from the couples.

"Listen, don't pay any attention to them. Can't you see they're looking for a fight?"

"Yeah, I know, but I ain't taking any crap from them."

Paul and Irene entered the theater and sat near the front.

"Want some popcorn?" Paul asked.

"Oh, yes, popcorn and a Coke."

"Okay, I'll be right back."

* * *

As Paul headed back to his seat, he saw his friends in line getting refreshments.

"Hey Arvin, what's happening? How you guys doing?

"Okay, Paul. Hey, did you hear about what John Carlos and Tommy Smith did at the Olympics?" Arvin asked.

"No, what happened?"

"After they won their races, they got on the victory stand and raised their black-gloved fists in air during the playing of the U.S. national anthem to protest the conditions of blacks in America."

"They did? Man, that was choice. It's about time we did something like that. But they're going to catch hell when they return to the U.S.," Paul said. He thought the Olympians were bold and brave young men who used the world stage to protest the treatment of blacks in America. But their actions placed another wedge between whites and blacks in America and further damaged race relations.

As Paul stood near the aisle, three white males walked passed him. One bumped him hard and stared.

"Hey man, what the hell is wrong with you?" Paul asked.

"Same thing that's wrong with you, boy," one white boy said.

Paul grabbed the boy by his shirt and shoved him against one of the seats.

Arvin immediately pulled Paul away. "Cool it, Paul, not now. If anything happens later, we're with you."

"Thanks, man." Paul said as he undid his fists and returned to his seat.

"I'm getting scared," Irene said as she clutched Paul's arm tightly. "Some guy came over to me and said that he didn't know I liked black people. He said when he's finished telling everyone at school about this, I'll be an outcast and kicked off of the cheerleading team."

"Don't worry, baby, everything's cool."

Someone in a group of white boys sitting behind Irene and Paul threw a cup and hit Paul in the head. Paul jumped up from his seat and ran in the direction from where the cup was thrown. "Who the hell threw that cup?"

"I did, boy," a voice answered.

"Well, come out here and get your ass whipping," Paul shouted. Paul walked toward the group and someone ran and charged Paul, tackling him at the waist. Everyone looked around to see what the commotion was about. They stood up, disregarding the movie and ran frantically toward the exits.

Arvin and his friends went to Paul's aid, as Irene stood up and placed her hands over her open mouth. The scene was nearly a racial riot at full throttle. The ushers couldn't control it.

"Call the police! Call the police!" one usher said as he saw the mass of bodies lying on the floor.

The police arrived and finally gained control of the situation.

"Who started this mess?" a policeman asked.

Paul gathered himself and with a cut lip and torn shirt said, "They did. It started even before I got in the movie."

"What do you mean?" the policeman asked.

"They started making comments about my white date. Then someone from that group hit me with a cup."

"Okay, step aside," the policeman said. Turning to the white group that Paul pointed out, the policeman asked, "Is that right?"

One of the white boys said, "He's full of it. He's just paranoid because we stared at him and his girlfriend."

The policeman looked at Paul, and then at the group of white boys.

"I'm taking both of your names, so don't go anywhere. Are there any witnesses?" the policeman asked.

No one came forward.

"What's your name?"

"Paul Hodge."

"What's your name?"

"Tim Plesher."

"I want you two guys to leave – leave by different exits, and I'll be watching you," the policeman said.

Paul looked for Irene and said, "Come on, baby, let's go."

"You're bleeding." Irene said.

"Nothing but a little cut. I'm all right."

Upon exiting the movie, Paul spotted Arvin and his friends. "Hey, man, thanks for helping me out. I'll never forget this."

"I told you we had you covered." Arvin said.

Chapter 9

The near riot at the movies became the talk of the town in Becton. The local TV stations and radio shows covered it during prime time. It shocked many people because incidents of this type just didn't happen in Becton. Paul and Irene pushed on.

They sat together high in the bleachers at a basketball game. Irene had hurt her ankle a few days before and couldn't participate as a cheerleader.

"Those cheerleaders look sloppy out there without you," Paul said.

"Oh, you're so sweet. Gimmie a kiss."

Paul kissed Irene on the lips and when he turned around to look at the game, it appeared that every eye in the gymnasium was focused on them.

"What the hell are you all looking at?" a defiant Paul yelled at a few onlookers nearby. There was no response.

* * *

After the game, Paul and Irene drove to their regular secluded spot where they cuddled while listening to Etta James's hit tune, "At Last." Irene nestled under his arm as he drove slowly. They stopped the car and stared at the stars in the sky. The crickets were loud that night and the breeze was cool. They were very comfortable around each other. As usual, Irene broke the silence.

"Wouldn't it be nice if the world could get along like us?"

Paul looked at Irene, slowly pushing aside her long black hair from her face and said, "Hell, I'd settle for just whites and blacks getting along in *this* country first; then we can work on the world."

"You're right on, Paul." Irene planted a kiss on Paul's cheek. They continued to embrace and listen to the cool music on WNJR.

* * *

A week later Ms. Cooper, a white physical education teacher, called Irene to her office. Ms. Cooper always wore black slacks which gave her a manly appearance. She was stern in her approach and left no doubt about her position.

"Irene, I called you into my office because I have a situation which I must rectify. You haven't participated in any cheerleading practices for three weeks now."

"Yes, I know. My ankle is still sore," Irene responded.

"I understand, but your absences are disrupting the practices. I need the full number of cheerleaders now; therefore, I'm afraid that I must replace you."

Irene stared directly into Ms. Cooper's eyes, not batting an eyelid. After a few seconds she leaned over on Ms. Cooper's desk and said, "They got to you, didn't they? This isn't about needing another cheerleading body; this is about my boyfriend, Paul. This is about racism."

"Irene, why are you talking this way? It has nothing to do with your black boyfriend."

"Yes, it does, yes, it does. Well, I like him, he likes me, and we're going steady. So, if you don't want me on the team, it's your loss." Irene abruptly got up from the chair and headed to her next class.

Paul saw Irene in the afternoon and noticed she wasn't her bubbly self. "What's the matter? Is there something wrong?"

"Ms. Cooper cut me from the cheerleading team. She said my absences were disrupting practices, so she replaced me, permanently."

"Ain't that a bitch? Oh, that's low down," Paul said with his lips formed tightly. "It's all about that fight at the movies, and the word is getting around about us."

"Well, I have you, and that's all I want."

"Yeah, baby, we have each other," Paul said as he smiled. He placed his arm around Irene's shoulders and walked off.

* * *

Paul and Oscar attended a birthday party for one of Oscar's friends. The disk jockey played one of Paul's favorite slow songs, "Oh, What A Night," by the Dells. Paul jumped up to look for a dance partner. There were plenty of pretty girls there so Paul had his pick. He eased over to a cute coffee-and-cream-complexioned young lady, with a short red skirt. She batted her eyelids and had one hand on her full hips as Paul approached her.

"Hey, baby, care to dance?" Paul asked.

"No thanks," the young lady replied.

Paul knew the rule to never ask a female from the same group of girls to dance where one had rejected him. So he went to another group of young ladies. He approached a cute, shapely legged girl who looked the other way as he came toward her.

"May I have this dance?" Paul asked.

"No," the young lady responded and started walking away from him.

"Hell, the record will be over before I get a dance." He went to a third group of young ladies and selected one. As he stuck out his hand, Paul asked, "Are you ready to boogie?"

"Yeah, but not with you. Where's your white girlfriend? That's who you need to find," the girl said.

Paul stood there, embarrassed, with his hand still fully extended. He dropped his hand and turned around, looking for Oscar.

"Oscar, all these chicks apparently know I'm dating Irene because they all refused me. I never got this many rejections before at a dance. Can you believe that shit?"

"Yes, I can. These black chicks ain't gonna forget that you made a grave switch to a white girl. They ain't gonna forget that."

"Okay, man, get me outta here quick. I don't have to take this. Let's go," Paul demanded.

Just as they got ready to leave, a guy walked up to them and asked, "Are you Paul Hodge?"

"Yeah, what's happening, man?" Paul responded already on edge.

"That white chick you're messing with must be doing you right. I don't know how you deal with the daily stares, insults, and other bullshit. She must be something else on the sheets."

"Yeah, your mother is something else on the sheets, too."

Both boys almost came to blows, but several people got between them. Paul and Oscar left the party and went home.

* * *

Paul called Irene. "Well, nothing else in our relationship can go bad now. I went to a party and got it from the blacks about our affair. I'm kind of glad it happened now rather than later. But I want to remind you that it's not over yet. It's going to happen again and again."

"It'll be worth it as long as we have each other. We're both strong, and we'll overcome this. They'll get used to seeing us together, you'll see. Don't sweat it."

CHAPTER 10

Paul sat down at the kitchen table while Mrs. Hodge fixed a western omelet, home-fried potatoes, Polish sausage, and prepared cinnamon apple sauce. He sipped a cup of freshly brewed Colombian coffee. He went to the door, retrieved the daily newspaper, and returned to the kitchen table. Paul turned to the sports page when suddenly his mother interrupted his train of thought.

"Son, I got a call yesterday from that girl's father."

Paul slowly lifted his head from the newspaper, and asked, "What girl?"

"The white girl you took up with. I didn't tell your father because he would have been real upset by some of the things that girl's father said."

Paul angrily pushed the newspaper aside. His lips tightened. "Well, what did he say?"

"He wants me to talk you into staying away from his daughter and to mingle with your own kind."

"He's got a lot of nerve. He should ask his daughter about who pursued who. I mean, Mom, she's aggressive and came after me. After awhile, I liked her ways and she grew on me. It's too late – we care for each other now."

"But, son, he said that if you don't stop seeing his daughter, he knows people in high positions who could make it hard on us. He didn't explain, but your father and I have worked too hard and too long to keep good relations with the white people. We don't want any trouble."

"Mom, that's called intimidation. That's what they use in the South to keep black people in line. You come from another generation, Mom, and I'm not taking that stuff. I'm sorry, Mom, I just am not going to take it."

Paul placed his arms around his mother's shoulders and said, "Don't worry. Everything will be all right."

Mrs. Hodge bowed her head and squeezed Paul's hands.

* * *

Paul made a sandwich as he watched *I Spy*, featuring Bill Cosby. The phone rang – it was Irene. "Have you heard the news?"

"No, now what happened?"

"Bobby Kennedy was murdered today in Los Angles. They got the guy who shot him."

"Well, I'll be damned. They're killing everyone on our side. When are they going to stop killing our leaders? Man, black people are in real trouble now." Paul sighed.

"Wow, we've lived during the murders of John Kennedy, Dr. King, and now Bobby Kennedy and we're not even out of high school. This is crazy," Irene said.

"Yeah, and it's all about white oppression of black people and wiping out anybody who attempts to help us. John Kennedy was starting to do some good things; Bobby showed black people he was on our side when he was U.S. Attorney General, and no telling how much more Dr. King would have led us."

"Wow, now they're all gone," Irene said sadly.

"Well, I'm getting involved. I feel myself getting very bitter about what's been happening. When I go to college next year, I'm joining some of those groups that are fighting for my civil rights."

"You should, Paul, because I'm thinking of doing the same thing."

"You *are*?"

"Yes. I must confess that I've been concerned about how black people have been treated. I feel guilty because I'm white and I'm one of the privileged ones. I think black people are beautiful people and deserve better treatment."

Paul was silent as he absorbed what Irene had just said. "Outta sight, Irene, I hope you do get involved. We can use a smart, aggressive person like you. By the way, I have something to tell you."

"What is it?"

"Your father called my mother the other day and asked her to tell me to leave you alone. He said if I continue seeing you, he'll make it hard on me and my parents."

"He did *what*? What the hell is wrong with him?"

"The pressure on us is getting rough. Do you still want to go steady?

"Oh, yes, Paul. I want nothing more in life."

"Fantastic. Let's keep doing what we've been doing. We're only a few months from graduation and being independent. We can make it. I'll see you tomorrow after second period."

* * *

As the bell rang for the end of the second period, Paul walked briskly to meet Irene.

Oscar called out, "Paul, where you going in such a rush?"

"Hey Oscar, what's happening?"

"Where you hustling to?"

"I'm going to meet Irene."

"Oh. How's it going?"

"A little rough, but we're both game."

"Keep truckin. She's a hip chick."

"Later, Oscar."

Paul and Oscar separated when Paul saw Irene standing by the auditorium. There was a group of white boys and girls standing nearby. Paul walked up to Irene and kissed her on the lips and she returned the kiss. That action turned everyone's head.

"Oh, look at the cute interracial couple," one white girl said. "Are you guys getting married and having some half-breeds?"

"Well, dude," said a white boy. "I've got to give it to you. You've got more nerve than Jesse James, kissing a white girl in front of us. Your luck is gonna run out."

Another white boy shouted, "You're a traitor to the white race, Irene."

Paul grabbed Irene and tried to walk away from the incident, but a boy who had been following closely behind smacked Paul in the back of his head. Paul twirled and hit the boy with a devastating right-hand punch, knocking him to the ground. The blow to the boy's chin sounded like a watermelon being dropped onto a concrete sidewalk. Blood flew everywhere; students started scrambling and several white boys had Paul in a headlock. Mass confusion followed. Several teachers broke up the fight and demanded to know what happened. By that time all within earshot of the commotion flocked to the scene.

Mr. Byrd, one of the teachers who arrived first, asked Paul to explain what happened.

"I was talking to my girlfriend and some of these people started making racial comments. I attempted to walk away but one of these turkeys slapped the back of my head. I turned around and swung at the person nearest to me and hit this guy."

Mr. Byrd asked the white group to explain their version of the incident.

A white boy stepped forward and said, "We didn't do anything. That black guy just started swinging."

"Okay," Mr. Byrd said. "Break this up and go to your classes. Paul, you come with me."

"For what?" Paul asked.

"Just come with me."

"What about those guys?"

"We just want to ask you some questions."

Paul looked at Irene, blew a kiss and went with Mr. Byrd.

"The principal must be informed of this incident so we're going to his office. What's that girl's name you blew a kiss to?" Mr. Byrd asked.

"Irene Dudash."

"Oh, I see, and she's your friend?"

"She's my *girlfriend*." Paul responded proudly.

"Oh?"

"Yeah, *Oh*." Paul responded sarcastically.

They entered Mr. Kelly's office and sat down. After Paul explained the incident and Mr. Byrd told what he had heard, Mr. Kelly looked at Paul and said, "I'm suspending you from school until you bring your parents in for a discussion about your behavior."

"Are you going to suspend the other guys, too?"

"No, not at this time."

Paul jumped from his seat and pointed his finger at Mr. Kelly. "This is bullshit. They started it and you're going to let them slide? That's what I call racism. It's because I'm dating Irene Dudash, isn't it?"

"No, it isn't, but I know I'll never convince you of that." Mr. Kelly looked down at his desk, needlessly shuffling papers.

"You're damn right you won't convince me," Paul said as he quickly exited the office.

"Now, here now, young man, watch your mouth and respect your elders."

Paul peeked back into the office. "I will when you respect my rights and the rights of my people." Mr. Kelly looked at Mr. Byrd and slowly closed the door behind Paul.

* * *

"Paul, what were you thinking of when you kissed that white girl in front of that group? What did you expect to happen?" Paul's father asked.

"I was just being me. I didn't think anything of it."

"Well, everything you do around these people is scrutinized. It almost sounded like you were rubbing it in their faces," Paul's father said.

"Dad, whose side are you on? No, I didn't try to rub it in their faces," Paul responded.

"Okay son, I'm not pleased that I have to take off from work, but I'm going to get you back in school. You can't afford to miss any more school time because you have to prepare for college."

"Thanks, Dad."

Paul called Irene and told her that he had gotten suspended for the fight.

"You mean to tell me those other people weren't suspended, too? *They* started it."

"I know, I know but that's the racism in this school and in this city. The sooner I get this behind me the better I'll be. I don't want my high school record messed up by this one incident."

"Well, it will be, won't it?"

"Maybe not. Maybe my parents can talk them out of placing this incident on my record."

"I hope so, because you are innocent."

CHAPTER 11

Paul's mother and father followed him into Mr. Kelly's office. Mr. Byrd also attended the meeting. The silence in the room was biting and uncomfortable. Everyone awaited Mr. Kelly's lead.

Looking directly at Paul's parents, he said, "Mr. and Mrs. Hodge, I can tell you care about your son by your presence here this morning and I applaud you for that. However, your son hit another student, and we do not condone that type of behavior at this school. We had to suspend him and make him responsible for his actions. Do you have any comments?"

Paul's mother started to say something, but his father interrupted her by placing his hand on her lap.

"Mr. Kelly, where are the other students that were involved in this fight?"

"They're not here because your son hit another student."

"With all due respect, sir, anyone knows that there are two sides to every story and I would like to hear the other side."

"Well, we're only dealing with what your son did on school grounds during school hours. My special assistant, Mr. Byrd, told me the entire story."

"Oh? Mr. Byrd, were you there?" Paul's father asked.

"Well, no, but the students told me the whole story, although I arrived right after it happened."

"So, you believe the other student's story over my son's version, is that right?"

"Yes," Mr. Kelly said as he slammed his hand on the table.

"Well, I've given both of you a chance to explain why my son was suspended and why the other students were not and why the others are not present here this morning. The only conclusion I can deduce from this is that it smacks of racism."

"What did you say? Are you calling us racists?"

"I'm saying the decisions applied in this incident are racist. You administer the decisions, so you figure it out," Paul's father replied.

Paul was surprised and proud that his dad was standing up to the school officials. Paul's mother was a silent observer.

"Mr. Hodge, I'm going to act like I didn't hear that response. Do you want your son to graduate this year?"

"Yes, and he will graduate with this incident wiped from the record because, do you know why? I will talk to my attorney about this issue and take the necessary legal actions against you and this school if my son isn't immediately re-instated in this school and any record of this incident wiped clean."

Mr. Kelly and Mr. Byrd looked at each other in bewilderment. They huddled and whispered a few words.

"Well, Mr. Hodge, we don't want to get the legal community involved in this matter. I'm sure we can work this out. Now, I'm going to let this issue slide. Paul can come back to school tomorrow and there will be no demerits or mention of this incident on his record. Is that satisfactory to you, Mr. Hodge?"

"That's fine with us. You have shown that you are a reasonable man. Thank you, Mr. Kelly."

Mr. Kelly rose from his chair and shook Paul's parents' hands. The Hodges exited the office with a look of satisfaction upon their faces.

* * *

"How'd it go?" Irene asked as she straightened out the telephone cord.

"Great. My dad was fantastic. He made Mr. Kelly and Mr. Byrd listen to reason. I think the threat of a law suit cleared up Mr. Kelly's mind."

"Have you told Oscar?"

"No, I'll call him later."

"Okay, call me later."

* * *

Paul walked into Herb's Sweet Shoppe, the only black hangout in town for teenagers. There were several girls at the entrance, talking and giggling as Paul approached.

"Hi, handsome," one of the girls said.

"Hi," Paul responded.

Before he could get through the entrance, a tall attractive girl with long black hair stepped in front of him and said, "What's the matter, you don't like dealing with the 'sisters' anymore?" She turned and faced a group of young ladies standing against the wall. "Ladies, I don't know if we're good enough for Paul. He likes those white girls because they do the nasty to him."

"Why don't you girls stop that stuff and stay out of my business. I don't want any more trouble."

"Well, well, well," a second girl said. "You already got trouble hanging with that white girl. There's always someone like you who jumps over to that white world, thinking the grass is greener. How can you stomach facing your brothers and sisters?"

Paul's attitude changed. His lips tightened and he frowned.

"You chicks don't know me so get off my back. All of you need to get a life."

CHAPTER 12

Two national events became of interest to Paul, one positive and the other negative. He thought about them as he pondered what was going on in America.

One event that bothered Paul was the election of Republican Richard M. Nixon to be the next President.

"Hell, Republicans care more about furthering rich people's causes than helping to improve race relations and the condition and treatment of minorities," Paul said out loud.

"I'm glad that I witnessed Shirley Chisholm become the first black woman to be elected to the Congress of the U.S. Man, this really is history."

* * *

Paul picked up Irene about eight o'clock in the evening and they headed to their special hideaway. A new song by South African trumpet player Hugh Masekela, "Grazing in the Grass," was playing on the radio.

"How do you like this song?" Paul asked.

"I like it, but how would you dance to it?" Irene asked.

"Beats me, but I like it, too. You ever hear of Miriam Makeba?"

"No."

"Well, that's his wife and she's a good singer. They both escaped the racist apartheid system in South Africa to be U.S. citizens."

"You know, I think that's why I dig you. You seem to know everything."

Paul stopped for a red light. He casually looked to his left and spotted two white police officers. When the light turned green, he pulled off slowly, being extremely careful not to exceed the speed limit or commit any traffic violations. He drove another ten blocks and noticed the patrol car was following them. Paul decided to abandon his original destination. He gave a right signal and turned down Laurie Street, a narrow side road.

"Paul, where are you going? You should be going straight."

"Two white officers are following us, so I'm not going to our regular spot. I'm going around the block and get back on the main road in case something happens."

"I'm scared," Irene said, leaning on Paul and peeking through the passenger side mirror.

"Yeah, we both should be with the way things are happening. Okay, they're making their move. They've turned on their patrol lights. Damn it, I knew they were going to stop us. Just be cool."

Paul pulled to the curb and kept his hands on the steering wheel in full review of the police officers. One officer shined the spotlight on his tags while the other, with his hands on his revolver, walked carefully and slowly to Paul's side of the car, stopping at the rear door.

"Let me see your license, registration, and proof of insurance."

"Yes, sir. May I go in my wallet to get my license?"

"Go ahead, and hurry up."

Paul got his license and asked, "May I open up the glove compartment to get the registration and insurance card?"

"Go ahead," the policeman said.

Paul handed the license, registration, and insurance card to the officer. Irene trembled as she looked straight ahead.

Twenty minutes after being stopped, the officer returned Paul's information and said in a harsh voice, "Get out, place your hands on the top of the car, and spread your legs. Lady, you wait behind the car."

The officer patted down Paul thoroughly. "You get over there in front of the car." The officer went to the back of the car and looked Irene over good. He immediately turned hostile.

"What the hell are you doing with this guy? Where the hell you going?"

Irene bit her lower lip and with her heart pounding said, "Just riding."

"Just riding where?"

"Just riding."

"You know a pretty little thing like you shouldn't be with his kind. Your parents know you with him?"

"Yes, they do."

The police officer changed his tone and shouted, "The hell they do! Look, we ain't letting no white girl date black boys in this town. This better be the last time I see you with him or the likes of him."

Irene trembled. "Hell, we weren't bothering anyone. Why did you stop us, because I'm white and he's black?"

"You better shut up or I'll haul your asses in."

"Go ahead. When you get ready to book us at the station, whatcha gonna write down? Huh? Huh? We've done nothing wrong."

The officer walked over to Paul and said, "Boy, I better not see you with this girl again or you gonna be in big trouble. Now you get the hell outta here."

Paul and Irene and drove off. He had an idea of who put the police up to tailing them.

"Are you okay?" Paul asked.

"Yes, but I'm shaken."

"Yeah, I am, too. You've got to do something for us."

"What?" Irene asked.

"I believe it was your father who got the police to tail us. Ask your father to back off because he could have gotten us killed tonight. Those were some nasty racist police officers."

"I think it was my dad, too. I'll talk to him later. I want him to understand the danger he put us in."

"Well, give it a try. I don't think we should be seen in the car together until you talk to your father."

"That makes sense."

* * *

Paul rushed home after dropping Irene off. He called Oscar and explained what had just happened.

"Man, you're lucky to be alive. They could have shot you on general principle. Paul, when are you going to realize that you're dealing in hazardous material with Irene? Is it worth it?"

"Damn right. Man, she's cool as hell. There ain't no sisters in this town as hip and as cool as Irene. I don't know where she gets it from. She's it, man. She's it."

Chapter 13

Paul and Irene sat on a bench at a public park to discuss prom plans. This year's prom was to be held at a new Four Seasons, a five-star hotel. It would be televised, as an experiment coordinated by the school and a local TV station. The students and school officials were excited about the experiment. Paul knew what he wanted to do – take Irene to the senior prom. It was their last year and he wanted it to go out with a bang. He didn't care what anyone thought.

The birds danced in and out of the park fountain, tweeting loudly as they flew by; squirrels picked up nuts, standing momentarily on their hind legs to crack several. Paul looked Irene in the eyes and said, "You know, the prom is coming up. I want you to go with me."

"Whoooaaaa. Are you sure you want to do this?" Irene asked.

"Hell, yes, this is our time, right now. What's the matter, don't you want to go with me?"

Irene hesitated for a moment, smiled, and said, "Of course, but I wonder if anything's going to happen?"

"We can't worry about that because it's out of our control."

* * *

Irene approached her father who sat in his favorite chair watching the *Rowan and Martin's Laugh-In.*

"Hi, Sugar. How ya doin?" Irene's father asked.

"Dad, something happened the other night that we need to talk about."

Irene's father sat upright in his chair as if something were sticking him in his butt and said, "What's the matter?"

"Did you have the police tail Paul and me?"

Irene's father bowed his head for a second and raised it immediately. "I did it for your own sake, sugar."

"Well, you almost got us shot."

"What?" Irene's father asked, rising quickly from his chair.

"The police officers were mean-spirited and racist. They said racist things to Paul and me and gave us a hard time. Look, Dad, this is not going to stop Paul and me from seeing each other so you might as well call them off."

"Sugar, I think you're making a big mistake, going around with that black kid. There're plenty of good red-blooded white boys in Becton. Your life is going to be limited if you continue to be seen with him."

"I'll take my chances. I'm asking you to call off the police."

"Okay, Sugar, I'm only calling them off because I don't want you to be harmed. I'm sorry I tried that approach. But you have to watch yourself because they still may come after you kids."

"Oh, thank you, Dad. Thanks for understanding."

* * *

Paul went to Barney's Clothing Store to pick out a tuxedo. He wanted to be sharply dressed. This prom required special attention. He ordered a lavender-colored tux with black lapels to replace the traditional white and black colors. He also selected a four-buttoned double-breasted tux to replace the traditional two-buttoned ones. Paul ordered a black feathery boutonniere and a white four-peaked pocket handkerchief for his jacket. Black shiny leather shoes topped off his outfit. He was set!

* * *

It was Monday evening, four days before the Friday prom.

"Hi, baby, what's happening?" Paul asked.

"Nothing now, but everything's going to be real gone Friday," Irene responded.

"Are you nervous?" Paul asked.

"Hell, yes, but I'm excited, too. What about you, and don't bullshit me."

"Well . . . ."

"Say no more, you're messed up, ain't you?" Irene asked.

"No, let's just say I'm looking forward to it. Hey, what are you wearing Friday?"

"It's a surprise. What about you?"

"It's a surprise."

"Okay smartass." Irene retorted. "Let's just surprise the hell out of each other." Paul and Irene choked with laughter.

"I'll see you at school," Paul said.

"Okay."

* * *

Paul picked up his outfit after school and headed home. He tried it on again to show his parents how impressive he would look for the prom.

"Son, that's a nice outfit but you ain't as sharp as I was when I went to my prom," Paul's father said as he winked. "And I had a pretty date, too."

"Oh?" his mother asked, smiling broadly.

"Are you taking that white girl?" Paul's father asked.

"Yes."

"Well, be careful."

"Dad, I hope you don't have any plans for Friday because I need the car."

"Oh, no, it's yours. Just replace the gas you use."

"I will."

* * *

Paul's phone rang. "Hey man, this is Oscar. I'm taking Pearlie to the prom Friday. You want to double date?"

"No, we better not."

"Why, something wrong?"

"Look, man, I'm taking Irene. I don't want to drag you into this controversy and you know there will be a lot of it Friday."

"Yup, I know what you mean. Plus, Pearlie wouldn't go for that anyway. She doesn't like white girls who date black guys. Be careful, man. This ain't gonna be no cake walk."

"Yeah, man. Thanks for the advice. Later."

* * *

Paul had difficulty sleeping that evening as he thought about the big Friday event. He planned for each possible scenario – name-calling, articles being thrown at them, physical violence. He knew he had to be cool or there would be big problems. He tossed and turned until day break.

Paul turned on the TV to get the weather report for Friday. "Friday will be mild and warm with no precipitation in the forecast," the meteorologist announced.

Thursday came very fast and Paul was only one day away from his big day with Irene.

"Hey, baby, how you doing?" Paul asked.

"Excited and awaiting our special day," Irene responded.

"Look, I told my parents about escorting you to the prom. They're okay with it and just asked me to be careful. Are you going to tell your parents?" Paul asked.

"Well, I wasn't going to tell mine. But do you think they'll see us on TV?"

"Oh hell, I forgot about it being televised. You'll have to take that chance. How are you going to get out of the house all dressed up with no escort?" Paul asked.

"My Aunt Gertie is the only member of my family I really can talk to. I've told her all about you and she likes what she's heard. You can pick me up at her house, at 22 Randle Circle. I'm going to tell my parents that I'm going to the prom from there with one of my girlfriends."

"Okay, sounds like a winner. I'll be there at eight o'clock."

* * *

Friday finally arrived leaving Paul and Irene's historic day but three hours away. He dressed early, paced the floor and looked at himself in the mirror at least one hundred times. He pranced back and forth, even stopping several times to pose like a model walking on a runway. His outfit was stunning and he knew it. A special outfit for a special day, accompanied by a special girl, he thought. He looked at his Bulova watch and it read seven o'clock. "Showtime – Our time – Time to go!" Paul shouted.

Paul pulled into the driveway at 22 Randle Circle. It was a small beige brick house with a perfectly manicured lawn; beautiful red and white azaleas lined the sidewalk, and on the front porch lay a lovely welcoming mat that deserved a design award for originality. Paul rang the door bell.

"Hello, you must be Paul," Aunt Gertie said.

"I am," Paul responded grinning and extending a handshake.

"Come right in, Paul, and have a seat. Irene will be with you soon."

"Thank you, Ma'am."

Irene finally exited the bedroom and headed to the living room where Paul waited. She stopped in her tracks when she saw Paul. She looked and looked and smiled broadly.

Paul slowly rose from the couch and stared at Irene from head to toe. "Baby, you look outta sight." Paul said.

"Wow, you don't look so bad yourself."

"Listen," Aunt Gertie said, "I want you kids to go out there and enjoy yourselves. This is the time of your lives that only comes around once, so don't allow anyone to ruin it. Now, Paul, you take good care of my little Irene."

"I will, Aunt Gertie, I will."

As they drove away, Irene leaned over and turned on the radio. Out came the sounds of Jerry Butler's "For Your Precious Love."

"Wow, this is so relaxing, Paul. I feel better already and it's making my nervousness disappear. How about you?"

"Baby, this is great. I'm ready for a boss evening."

Paul arrived at the hotel parking lot and exited the car. He helped Irene out and they headed to the ballroom, locked arm in arm. One hundred yards away, approximately 200 people lined up on both sides of the walkway to the entrance. Fifty yards away, a large number of TV trucks and cameras lined the crowded streets. Bright lights consumed the area and focused on the prom goers.

Paul and Irene strolled along, looking at each other. "Are you ready for this?" Paul asked.

"Are you ready for this?" Irene asked.

They smiled at each other, and before long they were finally in everyone's presence.

The groans and "oohs" and "aahs" started as people were shocked at what they were witnessing. A TV commentator stuck a microphone in Irene's face and asked, "Are you trying to make a statement of sorts? What prompted this arrangement?"

"What arrangement?" Irene asked.

"Well, is this your boyfriend?"

"Yes, he is."

"What are you trying to say?" Paul asked.

"Nothing," the commentator said. "I'm just trying to get some background here."

Irene brushed by him only to have a second commentator aggressively ask, "What do your friends think of you, dating out of your race?"

Paul leaped in with a response. "None of your damn business and get that microphone out of our faces."

By that time, they were in front of the heart of the crowd. The oohs and aahs continued more frequently until someone yelled out, "Why don't you go back to Africa along with your white traitor bitch?"

Paul and Irene kept walking, looking straight ahead, and trying to ignore the taunts and insults.

Even the few blacks that peppered the crowd threw out some of their own. "You settin us back one hundred years, brother. How are you gonna live with yourself?" a base voice echoed.

A female voice chimed in, "I'm cutting you back, Paul. I never thought you'd go for a white chick."

Suddenly, Irene screamed, "Ow, something hit me in the eye Paul."

"What?" Paul asked.

"My eye, I've been hit in the eye." Irene said. A small bag of rice lay at Irene's feet.

Paul grabbed Irene around her waist and ran through the doors. Irene began sobbing uncontrollably.

"Are you okay, baby?" Paul asked. "Here, let me see your eye."

A large red welt developed under Irene's eye.

"Those cowardly bastards!" Paul shouted. He ran out the door and stood in front of the crowd, with his fists balled up. "Who threw that bag of rice? Come on out here, you coward, because I'm gonna whip your ass."

The jeers kept coming, but no one claimed rights to throwing the bag of rice. Paul turned and ran back to Irene. The welt was larger and had started puffing.

"Baby, you're injured. I've got to get you back to Aunt Gertie's to put some ice on your eye because it's getting nastier looking every second."

"But, Paul, I don't want to ruin our special night. It'll be all right," Irene responded with soft, spasmodic sobs.

"Baby, I've made up my mind. We'll wait a few minutes until the crowd dies down and then leave."

Paul walked Irene off the large dance floor to a chair in the corner. "Wait here. I'll be right back."

Paul looked for Mr. Kelly. He spotted him in the corner in conversation with one of his teachers. Paul walked quickly to him and without excusing himself said, "Did you hear what happened?"

Mr. Kelly looked at Paul with mouth open and eyebrows raised. "No! What's wrong?"

"Someone from the crowd hit my date in the eye with a bag of rice and her eye is swollen. Can you call the police?"

"Where is she?"

"Right over here."

Paul walked quickly over to Irene and stopped while Mr. Kelly walked past them. "Mr. Kelly, we're over here, over here!" Paul shouted as he waived his hands frantically.

Mr. Kelly's mouth flew open, and asked, "Is this young lady your date for tonight?"

"Yeah, look at her eye. This doesn't make any sense."

"Yes, Paul, I see what you mean. Now, we don't want to get the police involved in this matter because, as you know, the prom is being televised and we don't want any bad publicity. We can put some ice on that eye and she'll be all right."

"But, Mr. Kelly, what about the coward that threw that bag of rice?"

"I'll go out and speak to the crowd about throwing things, but I don't think anyone is going to admit it. Let's leave it at that."

Paul looked at Mr. Kelly in disgust but said nothing. "Baby, we're getting out of here because the atmosphere ain't good for us. Nobody even came over to see if you're okay."

"I can feel my eye closing. It hurts, Paul. Wow, what a bummer."

The prom goers stared at them as they sat in the corner.

"Don't look now, baby, but they're staring at us. They don't know what to think. I think we shook them up," Paul said with a half grin. "You know, if we stayed, we would have won the 'best outfit' award. No doubt in my mind."

"We do look pretty snazzy. Where's Oscar?" Irene asked.

"I don't know. He's always late, so we may not see him. Listen to that music, baby. Didn't I tell you they'd play some lame music?" Paul looked at his watch. "Okay, let's get outta here."

They exited the hotel and headed to the parking lot. Only a handful of people remained from the large crowd. As they pulled out of the parking lot, Paul spotted Oscar's white 1965 Pontiac Catalina. He circled around, followed Oscar's car to a parking space, and pulled up beside it.

"Are you just getting here?" Oscar asked.

"Hell no, I'm just leaving." Paul responded.

Oscar turned off the engine, got out to help his date Pearlie, and went to Paul's car. "Why are you leaving so early?"

"Man, those racists threw a bag of rice from the crowd and hit Irene in her eye. Look at it – it's swollen like hell."

Oscar bent down to peep through Paul's driver side window and an angry frown appeared on his face. "Damn, that's messed up," he said. "I'm sorry to hear about this, Irene."

"Thanks for your concern, Oscar. We didn't feel comfortable staying, and my eye is getting bigger and bigger."

"I don't blame you guys for leaving. Anyway, we'll catch you guys later."

* * *

To Aunt Gertie's surprise, Paul and Irene arrived back at her house at around nine o'clock.

"Whatcha kids doing home so early?" she asked.

"It was awful, Aunt Gertie," Irene said. They threw a pack of rice, hit me in the eye. Look at it." Irene said, pointing to her eye, which now was closed shut.

"They did that to my baby? Those scoundrels!" Aunt Gertie said.

"Ms. Gertie, they ain't scoundrels, they're cold-blooded racists. They couldn't stand seeing us together," Paul said as he caressed Irene.

Irene looked at him and sheepishly nestled her head on his shoulders as she held an ice pack on her eye.

Chapter 14

"Hello, my little chickadees. This is WSTU and you're listening to the *Master Chic Show*. All of you know we have big fun cutting up and joking every day about life. Well, today I want to be serious, about an incident which occurred over the weekend at Four Seasons Hotel. For those who don't know what I'm talking about, a black boy and white girl decided to attend a prom together. While walking to the ballroom, someone threw a pack of rice at them and hit the girl in the eye. Racial epithets rained down on them from the crowd to complete the insult. In addition, apparently a near riot occurred at the local movies last week involving this same interracial couple when some people harassed them unmercifully.

"Today's show is dedicated to taking your comments about these unfortunate incidents," Master Chic said.

"You're on the air."

"I think it was disgusting to see that black boy with that white girl. The nerve of them! God didn't mean for the races to mix."

"Thank you, ma'am. You're on the air at WSTU. You're comment, please."

"We have to teach that black boy to stay with his own kind, and that goes for the white bitch, too."

"Okay, there'll be no cussing on this station. We run a clean show and we will not tolerate that type of language. We're going to a ten-second delay to cut out any cussing you make. So be considerate of those families that have small children around. Thank you in advance for your cooperation. You're on the air."

"I hear the white girl was hit in the eye with something while walking to the prom. She's lucky I wasn't there. I'd teach her something for messing with blacks."

"Thank you for your comment. Hello, you're on the air. Go ahead with your comments."

"I'm a white female. If that's what that young couple wants to do, so be it. There's no law against interracial dating in New York or in Becton. I hope Becton learns from this ugly incident that we all must learn to live together."

"Thank you, ma'am. You're on the air."

"The days are over when white America can tell us who to date, what we can say, where we can live, where to go to school, and so forth. You killed many of our leaders and you've tried to hold us down for hundreds of years. But we are a strong people and refuse to give up."

"Thank you, sir. You're on the air."

"I don't condone what happened at the prom but these kids should have known something negative was going to happen. I'm glad the girl's eye wasn't knocked out because that would have been a real tragedy. I'd like to know if the parents of these two kids knew they were dating and if they supported them."

An official from the local chapter of the National Association for the Advancement of Colored People in Becton called in. "The racial incidents at the prom have set race relations in Becton back twenty years. I couldn't believe the type of questions those TV reporters asked those kids. Clearly, they were biased in their reporting and lacked objectivity. And the person who threw the pack of rice, hitting that poor girl in the eye is a monster and a coward. This heinous crime should not go unpunished. School officials should have called the police and the fact that they didn't is reprehensible. Those who want to do things the old way by stomping on the rights of individuals need to read a law that protects people's civil rights. It's called the Civil Rights Act of 1964, as amended."

The calls kept pouring in until the show went off the air.

* * *

Paul's parents saw the TV broadcast that the Four Seasons and the high school had collaborated on. They confronted their son.

"Son," Mr. Hodge said with a frown, "you see what I mean? We don't need that type of problem. We've had discussions about the struggles of blacks in this country. You even told me you might join SNCC to fight for the civil rights of our people, yet you stirred up controversy by dating that girl. You appear to have two different allegiances – one for the white girl and the other for your race. Son, that's a dangerous and confusing dichotomy."

Paul stared at the floor. Sweat exuded from the pores of his forehead, and his legs quivered. His parents anxiously awaited his response.

"Oh geez, Dad, I don't know what to say. I still want to get involved with the struggle, but I also dig Irene. She's some kinda bad. I like her because she's a very independent-thinking girl. Dad, she even said she's going to get involved in our struggle when she goes to college. Can you imagine that, in *our* struggle? How many whites would do that? Not many!"

"Are you sure you're not mistaking her lust for you for her so-called desire to join the struggle?"

"Dad, that was a low blow."

"Well, I'm just . . ."

"Dad, I know this girl. She is for real, and I trust her."

"Do her parents accept you?"

"Her father doesn't and her mother, well, I don't know about what she thinks."

"I heard about what her father did, having you followed by the police. That's your lesson right there, Paul. Think about it. They don't want you with their girl."

Paul got up slowly off the couch and walked toward the hallway. He stopped, whirled around, and said to his parents, "I'm eighteen now and almost out of school. I don't think you'll ever agree with me about dating Irene so I'm not going to try to convince you."

"Okay, son, just be ready to handle the continued consequences of your decision."

Paul nodded and walked to his bedroom.

Chapter 15

Graduation time finally arrived, although Paul had mixed feelings about this important event. The excitement of moving on brought joy and anticipation. However, he also knew that he would have to part ways with Irene when they went away to college.

A few days before graduation, Paul and Irene walked slowly as they talked.

"Are you ready for the big day?" Paul asked.

"Yeah, I guess so."

"You don't sound too enthusiastic."

"I just have things on my mind."

"Is there some room in that brilliant mind to include thoughts of me?"

Irene smiled sheepishly, playfully poked Paul in the chest with her forefinger, and said, "Oh, there will always be plenty of room for you."

Paul smiled. "Hey, guess what I heard this morning. Everyone is talking about it."

"No, what?" Irene asked as she stopped walking.

"You won an award for accumulating the most extracurricular points in the school's history. Congratulations, baby," Paul said as he hugged her.

"Wow! I did? That's a much-cherished surprise and honor for me because I had no idea I was doing any such thing as establishing some kind of record."

"Well, I'm very proud of you, and I know your parents will be, too. Now, I have another surprise."

"Wow, you're full of surprises, aren't you?"

"I've been thinking about this one for some time. Look, our high school careers are just about over, and we've been through a lot together. We're both going off to college in a few months, and you'll be off to the Jersey shore to work for the summer. I thought it would be nice if we went to New York City to a jazz club, and maybe even a movie, to celebrate. We owe it to ourselves. What do you think?"

Irene grabbed Paul's arm, smiled, and said, "Oh, yes, yes, I would love to go."

"Okay. We'll go the day after graduation. You know, we always discuss rhythm and blues music, but I also want you to hear my type of jazz and Latin music or as they call it now, salsa. We'll go to the Village Vanguard, the Palladium, and the Cheetah Club. I know you'll love it."

"I can't wait."

* * *

As the seniors filed in the auditorium for graduation, Paul scanned the crowd. He spotted his parents in the balcony, and other friends, and family members on the lower level.

This is it, he thought, as he sat down. The girls entered, Irene near the end of the procession.

After a musical introduction, preliminary statements by the principal and a guest speaker, the principal acknowledged the outstanding students and presented them with awards.

"Paul Hodge, please approach the podium."

Paul blinked with surprise, then walked to the stage.

"Paul, you had a resounding track career at Becton High School and you are a diligent student. We want to present you with the 'Outstanding Student/Athlete of the Senior Class' award. Congratulations, Paul." The principal shook Paul's hand and gave him the award.

Applause.

"I thank my coaches, fellow track mates, teachers, and parents for helping me meet school standards for receiving this award."

"Have you decided where you'll be attending college in the fall, Paul?" the principal asked.

"Yes, I'll be attending Shaw University in North Carolina."

"Good. We'll be looking out for your accomplishments there as well."

Additional applause.

"Irene Dudash, please approach the podium."

Irene walked to the podium and smiled as she approached the principal.

"Irene, this is a very special award because, in my opinion, it may never be topped. Irene has received the most extracurricular points ever in the history of Becton High School. The award reads: 'To the student that excels in the most extracurricular activities during a high school career.' Congratulations, Irene." The principal shook Irene's hand and gave her the award.

Applause.

"Thank you, sir. I want to thank my fellow classmates, teachers, and parents for supporting me during my high school career, which enabled me to win this award."

Additional applause.

The graduation ceremony continued with the remaining students receiving awards and diplomas.

"Now go out into the world, learn everything possible, be motivated, never give up, and find good jobs to support your future families. The faculty of this school wishes you all the best of luck in the future," the principal concluded.

The graduates threw their caps into air. Their high school careers were behind them and new social, academic, and professional frontiers lay ahead.

Chapter 16

The next evening Paul kept his promise to take Irene to New York City. This was a new day. They weren't hiding any more, they were college-age, young adults.

In the city, they reached Paul's first stop, the Village Vanguard.

"Who is playing here tonight?

"Sonny Rollins and his group are featured. He's one of the top jazz saxophonists in the world. He started playing at the age of nineteen with jazz greats such as Charlie Parker and Bud Powell. I know you don't recognize these names, but, trust me, they were some of the top jazz musicians of all time."

"Well, it just goes to show you that there's always something new to learn about a person. I thought you only knew the rhythm and blues groups and songs. Wow! You're so talented."

They enjoyed the first set, then decided to leave. Paul took Irene to a Jewish deli for a pastrami sandwich on rye bread with Russian dressing and a little mustard.

Paul devoured his sandwich in a flash. "How do you like it?

"It was boss, but I'm afraid that I can't eat the rest of it. I'll take it with me to eat later. Where are we going now?"

"This is going to be very different. We're going to the famous Palladium Ballroom, where the best Latin bands perform and the best mambo dancers do their thing. I used to listen to the New York stations play this music and I fell in love with it. I visited this place many times and danced a little bit."

Paul and Irene headed to 53rd and Broadway to the Palladium. They were in luck. Two of the best bands were performing: Tito Puente and Tito Rodriguez.

The music began and Paul's fingers started tapping. "Do you mind if I dance with one of the ladies? I know you're not familiar with these dances."

"You're right. No, go right ahead."

Paul escorted a lady to the floor and danced to Tito Puente's hit, "Ran Kan Kan." He twisted and turned her as if they were old dance partners. The other dancers were expert innovators of the mambo and salsa dance styles. The song ended.

"I'm impressed. You were magnificent, and I see why you like this music. It's exciting and fun."

"Thanks. Come on – let's dance. I'll take it slow, so just follow me." After dancing awhile Paul said, "Let's go to the Cheetah Club. They really party there and it's only a block away. Are you ready?"

"Yes, Paul, yes. I'm having so much fun."

The Fania All-Stars were playing at the Cheetah Club. They were in luck again. The special night was being filmed and recorded, and the place was rocking. The Master of Ceremony, the legendary New York disk jockey, Symphony Sid, made the night even more exciting with his unique delivery in announcing various all-star musicians and their hit songs. The band played one of Paul's favorite songs, "Quitate Tu."

"Come on, baby, let's dance," Paul said.

The pulsing and staccato beat of the sixteen-minute song stimulated and intrigued Paul and Irene.

"Which movie would you like to see, *Planet of the Apes*, or *Valley of the Dolls*?" Paul asked.

"*Planet of the Apes*."

They took in the sights of New York and headed to the movies.

* * *

"I had a great time. Thanks for showing me around and exposing me to the different music and artists. Wow! It was something else. I'll never forget this trip."

"I won't, either. But let's really make it a memorable trip. Would you like to rape me? I promise that I will not call the police."

"Are you serious?"

"I'm serious as a heart attack."

"I've been ready for two years! I'm all yours!"

Chapter 17

The University of Southern California accepted Irene's application for enrollment in the fall of 1968. Paul made plans to enter Shaw University. Irene worked on the Jersey shore for the summer, and Paul stayed around the Becton area, hanging out with close friends.

They saw each other one last time before heading to college. Paul picked up Irene at a corner near her house. They headed to their regular spot while the popular song, "Hang On Snoopy, Hang On," by The McCoys, played. Paul pulled up to a secluded area and turned off the car lights. Neither one could see the other – it was pitch-black. Irene reached for Paul, and they kissed passionately.

"What am I going to do without you, Paul?"

"No, the question is what am I going to do without *you*. Baby, it's going to be hard, but it'll be all right. I tell you what. Let's make a promise right here and now to never stop seeing each other, regardless of our life status or situation. I'll start off. I, Paul Hodge, make that promise to Irene Dudash."

"I promise, too, Paul, I promise." They hugged the breath out of each other, kissed passionately, and made love.

* * *

That summer Paul had a serious conversation with Oscar about their future. Paul, wearing a white embroidered dashiki, with bell-bottom trousers covering his three-inch tan shoes, leaned against his father's blue 1965 Plymouth Valiant as Oscar walked up to him.

"What do you think life has in store for us, Paul?" Oscar asked.

"Well, for certain, we gotta boogie out of Becton to find out. I'm cutting out to Shaw University because I'm going to be comfortable learning at a black school. I think we've missed plenty socially by being raised in Becton. It's too "white" here. There's nowhere for black people to go, and we don't have anyone looking out for us. I'm blowing town."

"I don't want to go south," Oscar said. "Most of the good black schools are located in the South, but I ain't ready to tackle that Jim Crow stuff."

"Yeah, I know what you mean, man. Remember when we used to look down our noses at black Southerners, thinking we were better than them because we attended integrated schools? Well, look at us now. We're talking about visiting their states and towns to attend school. It's almost like two ships passing in the night – black Southern people going north in search of employment and integration, and Northern black youth going South to continue their education at black colleges. What a dynamic that is."

"But what do you *really* want to do in life, Paul?"

"I'd like to get a college education and work in New York City, Los Angeles, Chicago, or Washington, D.C. for a private company, in an executive capacity of sorts."

"But you might be drafted into the military first. This country is fighting in some place called Vietnam and they're drafting guys our age, especially blacks, to haul into the service to fight."

"Well, they can forget about me because I'm going to college. I'll be damned if I'm going to fight in some war when black people continue to be treated as second-class citizens in this country. Man, the racism in this country is something else. Look at how those bastards killed three Civil Rights workers in Mississippi who were attempting to register voters; how they murdered those four little black girls in Birmingham, Alabama; how civil rights worker Medgar Evers was slaughtered in the doorway of his home by a sniper, and what they did to Emmett Till in Mississippi. And they want us to risk our lives by fighting in some foreign war? That's just not right, Oscar. I'm going to get involved in our struggle somehow."

"Whatcha got in mind, Paul?"

"Well, I've been reading in the *New York Afro-American* newspaper about the Student Nonviolent Coordinating Committee. Do you remember me telling you about going to SNCC Headquarters at Shaw University last year? Well, I'm going to join them when I get in college. I saw how they operate and I liked it."

"Paul, you've got to be careful fooling around with those groups. Many of them are getting shot at and beat up by the crackers and police, alike."

"I'm not afraid of those crackers. They're wrong as hell. They want to keep our people down and work us to death for their own selfish benefit. My parents took the injustices and abuse but I'll be damn if I will. What about you, Oscar, are you willing to fight for your rights? You don't sound too concerned."

"I'm concerned, Paul, but I guess I'm not as aggressive as you."

"Well, you'd better start because conditions are not going to improve unless you get involved. Don't leave it for others to do – you do your part and let the chips fall where they may."

"Yeah, Paul, I guess you're right."

Chapter 18

The fall day was destined for beauty. The magnificent morning sunshine pierced a light blue sky, absent of any clouds. A light breeze made the morning almost perfect. Paul walked to the auditorium where Shaw University held freshman orientation. He felt strange in his new and different environment. The one thing that chilled his spine was that it appeared that ninety-eight percent of the people making their way to orientation with him were black. Unlike Becton High School, he didn't have to look for them – they were everywhere. It made him proud, confident and open-minded to a new and exciting educational and social experience. He didn't know anyone but kept looking for familiar faces. There were none.

As he sat down near the front of the auditorium, he caught the eye of a fellow freshman seated near him.

"Hey, what's happening? My name is Paul Hodge." He extended his hand.

"My name is Al Roundtree. Nice to meet you.

"Where are you from?" Paul asked.

"Englewood, New Jersey, and you?"

"Becton, New York."

"Where's that?" Al asked with a frown.

"Oh, it's about sixty miles northwest of New York City."

"You know where Englewood is?" Al asked.

"Yeah, I think it's near the George Washington Bridge. The Isley Brothers singing group used to claim it as their hometown, but I think they're originally from somewhere else. Man, they used to bring the house down with their hit 'Shout.'"

"Hey, man, I see you know your musical artists."

"I do all right. What dormitory are you staying in? Paul asked.

Al fumbled through his orientation information. "I'm in Benson Hall, room 303."

"I'm in the same hall, room 202."

Paul listened intensely to the orientation. He scanned the sea of black freshmen and couldn't help but wonder how many would graduate. He could only vouch for one person – himself.

A member of SNCC named Bentley Benton approached the stage and grabbed the microphone. His bush hairstyle extended one foot high and one foot wide on both sides of his head. He wore a yellow and blue paisley-colored dashiki and faded blue bell-bottom jeans that nearly covered his black, four-inch high heeled boots. He paced the stage four or five times, holding the microphone at his side, and scanned the audience for several minutes. People started hissing and clapping for action.

Bentley shouted out with a strained high-pitched voice, "Can any of you sisters or brothers tell me who Ella J. Baker was?"

Silence.

Bentley repeated his question.

Silence.

"I'm not surprised, but if you think I'm gonna let you off the hook, you might as well believe that I have beachfront property in Arizona to sell you," Bentley said. "Before you leave Shaw University, you *will* know more about whom she was, but for the purposes of getting you started, I'll tell you. She founded the Student Nonviolent Coordinating Committee, yeah, she did. She was a dynamic sister who graduated from this university in 1927 and dedicated her life to social justice. You need to read up on her. Now can you tell me how SNCC made history?"

Several hands went up.

"Yes, you sister, with the red vest."

"In 1960, four of its members sat at a segregated 'whites only' lunch counter in Greensboro, North Carolina and refused to leave when ordered to do so. It spawned similar sit-ins in other cities across the United States and helped challenge segregation."

"Good," Bentley said. "The only clarification I want to make is that, it was after that initial sit-in that SNCC was started and the effort helped organize students to go to other cities and states to protest segregation. We still need volunteers to help SNCC continue to fight all forms of segregation, help with voter registration, and fight white oppression.

"Okay, let me tell you about some of the people in the movement. John Lewis was the first Chairman from 1960 to 1966. He was a brave brother who got his ass beat many times by the police for marching against white oppression and segregation. He was replaced by a brilliant brother named Stokely Carmichael, but Stokely wanted to shoot up all white people and we couldn't have that. SNCC is a nonviolent organization and we had to get Stokely out of there. We're looking at a sharp dude named H. Rap Brown to lead us in 1969. We just lost a member of the SNCC family, a brother named Sammy Young, who was murdered by a white gas attendant for using a white bathroom. He was the first black college student to die in the Black Liberation Movement. And, with all that blacks are going through in this country, we ain't about to go and get shot up and killed in some country named Vietnam, fighting the white man's war. Sho-nuff, hell no!

"My brothers and sisters, you can learn more about SNCC by getting involved. It's for your future, as well as the future of your kids and grandkids. We need you now! Now, do we have any volunteers?"

Paul's hand shot up first and others followed. They kept popping up like mushrooms in a field. Forty more students raised their hands, including Al.

"All those who raised their hands, see me up front for registration and do it quickly," Bentley ordered.

Paul and Al hustled down front to register. Paul angled his way toward the front of the line, raised his hand, and caught Bentley's eye.

"Yes, what can I do for you, my brother?" Bentley asked.

"I volunteered last year. My cousin and I helped out with registration, and I went out in the field to observe how the sit-ins were done."

"Right On! We can use you. What's your name, my brother?" Bentley asked.

"Paul Hodge."

"Paul, come around to the other side of the table and I'll hip you to how we're doing registration this year."

* * *

Paul became an active member in SNCC, registering many of his fellow students and participating in several sit-ins in Alabama and North Carolina.

"Next," Paul said.

"Hi. My name is Henrietta and I want to register to volunteer."

"May I please have your full name?"

"Oh, my name is Henrietta Williams."

"Okay, Henrietta, I need to know your major, class schedule, and your availability on weekends to register voters and/or to participate in sit-ins here in North Carolina. Here is a pamphlet on what SNCC does at these activities and information on how you're supposed to conduct yourself. The buses will pick up volunteers at the administration building on the second and fourth Saturdays and Sundays of each month at nine o'clock a.m. sharp and drop you back at the same location at five o'clock p.m. This is no walk in the park, so if you have second thoughts, let us know. I also need to have a phone number for your nearest relative in case anything happens. Please wear this SNCC Volunteer sticker on your lapel. Any questions?"

"Yes. What are you doing later tonight?" Henrietta asked, smiling mischievously.

"Nothing. Write down your number. Maybe we can hook up." Henrietta wrote down her number and left the table. Paul gazed as she sashayed her voluptuous hips down the corridor. He nodded to what he was seeing and said, "Oh Yeah."

* * *

Several weeks went by; Paul and other volunteers were assigned to Williamston, North Carolina, a segregation stronghold just north of Greenville. While racial conditions were loosening up in several areas across the South, Williamston continued to challenge the Civil Rights laws.

Paul and two other volunteers, including Bentley Benton, walked into a restaurant, sat in a booth, and waited for a server. Ten minutes went by and Paul looked around to get someone's attention. No one came to the table. Everyone was ready to order.

"Paul, go up to the cashier and ask them why no one has come to our booth. Just be cool and firm," Bentley instructed.

Paul walked up to the cashier, who was fumbling with some bills and asked, "Can we please get some service at our booth?"

The cashier, a dirty-blond-haired skinny female with several decayed front teeth looked at Paul while chewing gum rapidly and saying nothing as she kept arranging the receipts on the counter.

"I'd like to talk to the manager," Paul said.

"He's not *here*," the cashier told Paul, staring out the window and never looking his way.

"Well, who's in charge?"

"Me."

"Do you have a name?"

The cashier stared at Paul, looking him up and down.

"My name is Beth."

"Beth, can we please get some service?"

"We'll get there when we can," Beth said, raising her voice. "We ain't doing nuttin special for you people."

Bentley slowly walked to the counter. He placed his hands in the front pockets of his brown and yellow pinstripe dashiki shirt. The customers seated nearby stopped eating. Bentley's large bush hairstyle was fully evident.

"Look here, Miss America, I know you can't read too well or you wouldn't have this minimum-wage-ass paying job, but you better get us some service right away or we'll close this damn place down."

"Who do you think you are? I'm calling the police," Beth said, her hands shaking as she started to dial the number.

"Good damn it, call them," Bentley demanded. "I know I'm wasting my breath, but have you heard of the Civil Rights Act of 1964? Of course you haven't. Well, let me give you a little history lesson, Miss America. The lily-white places you've had to yourself all these years are being 'rainbowed.' In other words you have to serve anyone who sits in your booths or at your counters – blacks, browns, yellows, purples – and do so in a manner equal to your white customers. Yeah, go ahead and call the police. I'm dying to see what they're gonna do when they get here."

The place got so quiet you could hear a rat piss on cotton. No one said anything for approximately two minutes. The stillness was awkward.

Beth slowly placed the phone back on the receiver and motioned to a waiter to serve the party at Bentley's table. Beth never said another word to Paul or Bentley.

The volunteers ate heartily. After boarding the bus, Bentley faced the volunteers with both hands held high above his head. "I did what I did to demonstrate to you all how to approach these bastards who still want to resist serving us. The Civil Rights laws are on the books. All we have to do is test them and if they resist serving us, we take them to court and make them pay and maybe close them down. You dig? Questions, anyone?"

No one questioned Bentley's aggressive approach, but there was plenty of buzz among the volunteers. The experience really impressed Paul. He reflected back on his high school days when he certainly could have used Bentley during the fight at the movies and the commotion at the prom.

* * *

Paul got Irene's phone number at Southern California University from Aunt Gertie.

"Hey, wonderful one. How are you doing?"

"Hi, handsome, I'm doing just fine. I wondered what happened to you and why you haven't called. I gave Aunt Gertie my phone number at school months ago. Is some Southern chick keeping you busy down there?"

"How did you know about her?" Pause. "Just kidding. No, really, I've been super busy with the books and SNCC sit-ins."

"Has SNCC been successful with its sit-ins?

"Oh, yeah. Some of us have been hurt by the police, but it's a small price to pay for equality. We're moving forward."

"Okay, Paul, but please be careful. I wish you could visit me on the 'left coast.' There are some wild folk out here but I'm lovin it. The weather is always great, I've made many friends, and I'm glad I made the choice to attend school here. My studies are coming along fine and I've even found to time to join the cheerleading squad. We have great basketball and football teams and I cheer for both."

"Sounds like Southern California is your kind of place. I'm glad it's working out for you there.

"Paul, do you miss me?"

"Hell, yes."

"Is that promise that we made to always see each other still hot?"

"Sizzling like a hot steak just off the grill, baby!"

Chapter 19

Paul graduated from Shaw University, returned to Becton, and began sending out job applications. He had a plan to work during the day and attend graduate school at night. His goal was to secure a master's degree in business administration and work in the corporate world.

"There's mail on the dining room table, Paul." Mrs. Hodge said.

Paul picked up the tan envelope and opened it. It was from the U.S. Selective Service. "What the hell is this?" Paul said.

He opened the one-page letter quickly. It read: "Mr. Paul Hodge, you are here-by requested to report to your local Armed Forces Center for induction into the U.S. Army. Your tour of duty will be for two years. Report promptly on June 24th at nine o'clock a.m. sharp."

Paul staggered to the couch and sat down, in slow motion, still staring at the letter. His mind went blank. Several moments went by.

Paul shouted, "Hell, no, I won't go. Not now. I've got plans for the future and they don't include the military."

Paul's mother came running into the room. "Paul, what's wrong?"

"Look at this, Mom," Paul said, showing his mother the formal letter. "I've been inducted into the U.S. Army, and I have to report in six weeks. They're messing up my future plans, and I ain't going."

Paul's mother looked at the letter and began weeping. "Paul, dear, I don't want you going into the army, either, but you'll be in big trouble if you don't report when they say report. You gotta go."

Paul grabbed his head with both hands. "But, Mom, they're gonna send me straight to Vietnam, I know they are. Fighting in this war is one of my worst fears."

"Son, your father and I will pray that they don't send you to Vietnam. We want you right here in Becton, but you must obey the law and report."

Paul went to his room and slammed the door. He picked up the phone and angrily called Oscar.

"Hey, man, this is Paul. Man, would you believe that the U.S. Army is calling me into service?"

"Aw, no shit, man. Aw, damn, Paul, that's cold. When do you have to report?"

"In six weeks, man, six weeks. I can't do shit in six weeks. Oscar, we talked about this bullshit of serving in Vietnam and it looks like I'm going to be living it."

"It's gonna be all right, Paul."

"Yeah, it's easy for you to say that. Man, I don't mind telling you, I'm scared as hell. Ain't too many of us brothers coming home in one piece from Vietnam."

"There's a chance you won't go to Vietnam, at least that's what I'm hoping. Now is the time to think positive, Paul, and get through this."

"Hey, I saw Irene last week and she asked about you. Man, she looked scrumptious. She's working on the Jersey shore again this summer. She should be home by now," Oscar said.

"So she looked good, huh? Damn, I gotta see her. I may have a lot to do before I report to basic training at Fort Hood, Texas, but nothing comes before seeing Irene."

Let's get tanked before you report," Oscar suggested.

"Right on, boss, let's do it."

* * *

Paul felt it was time to contact Irene. After all, he didn't know how many times he would see her before going off to the military.

"Hi, I have some bad news."

"What is it?" Irene asked.

"I've been recruited into the U.S. Army and I have to report in six weeks. Oscar and I were just talking about the possibility of one of us being recruited, and damn if it didn't happen to me."

"Oh, no, that's cruel. How are your parents taking it?"

"Not well at all. I told them that I wasn't going, but they talked some sense into my head. Well, getting that big-time job is going to be delayed for a few years. Man!"

"Well, you know I'm going to miss you very much. I've got some good news, though."

"I'm all ears."

I've been accepted for graduate school at Stanford University."

"That's great baby, I'm happy for you."

"One good thing is that I'll be so busy that I won't go crazy thinking about you all the time. But I feel bad because I know that you have plans to go to graduate school, too. Wow, I wish you didn't have to go into the military."

"Okay, let's be positive about this. We have two things to celebrate: your acceptance to graduate school and my leaving for the military. We may as well honor both events, right?"

"What did you have in mind?"

"Baby, we're going to a five-star hotel, order room service, get a bottle of good champagne, and love each other to death for a couple of days."

"Whoopie! Sounds like my kind of party, Paul."

CHAPTER 20

Paul and the other recruits got off the bus at Fort Hood, Texas and headed to the processing center. The temperature was already in the nineties. A platoon of sixty men marched by them in perfect cadence. As they marched, a drill sergeant shouted, "Left, right – go to your left right, left right, left right – go to your left right, left right."

"Ain't no use in going home. Ain't no use in going home. Jody got your girl and gone. Jody got your girl and gone. Sound off – one, two. Sound off – three, four. Take it on down – one, two, three, four, one, two, – three four."

They all got buzzed haircuts, supplies, and clothing and reported for orientation. This was a new day for Paul. He had to adjust to military life to make it run smoothly and he was ready for the challenge. Rising at four o'clock in the morning, walking ten miles daily, participating in bivouac exercises, kitchen police, and obsession with neatness of clothes and room were things he handled well.

Basic training ended – the time went by fast.

"Hey, does anyone know when the assignments are going to be posted. I'm glad we finished this basic training shit," a tall soldier said as he spit-shined his black boots.

"I heard they'll be out around four o'clock this afternoon," Paul said.

"Well, I'm ready to get out of here," the soldier said.

"Everyone, line up outside the barracks," the first sergeant shouted later that day. "Some of you are going to be disappointed, some of you will be glad, and some of you are going to be scared. You've had a great basic training and you'll be ready, wherever you go. Fall out and review your assignments. Good luck, men, and may God be your companion."

Paul ran to find his permanent assignment. He went down the list with his index finger, found his name and saw the word "Vietnam" beside it. He didn't believe what he was seeing. Again he placed his index finger on his name and again saw "Vietnam" beside it.

"Damn. Why me? Why me?"

A soldier placed his arm around Paul's shoulders and said, "Hey, man, I'm sorry, but you'll make it okay. Just trust your fellow soldiers to watch your back."

"Hey, man, thanks for your thoughts. I need to call my parents. This ain't going to be easy for them."

Paul returned to the barracks and called his parents. "Hi, Mom, how are you and Dad doing?"

"Okay, son. How are they treating you down there?"

"Fine, Mom. I finished basic training today and received my assignment."

"Are they assigning you close to home?"

"No, Mom, I'm going to Vietnam in two weeks."

"Oh no, son, oh no. Why you?"

"I don't like it, but that's just the way the ball bounces, Mom. I'll be okay. I've got to call Oscar. I'll see you next week."

Paul's mother tried to hold back from crying on the phone but her whimpers began to flow freely.

"Take it easy, Mom, don't cry."

"I can't help it. I'm already worried about you going to that god-forbidden place."

"Mom, I've got to go. I'll see you later."

Paul hung up the phone and called Oscar. "Hey Oscar, what's happening, man?

"Paul? Is this you, Paul? Man, how you doing? How are they treating you?"

"I'm being shipped to Vietnam. Can you believe this crap? We've talked and talked about Vietnam and now I'm headed there. What the hell is going on?"

"Aw, man, that's a bitch. Man, I don't know what to say. Damn, that's bullshit."

"I'm scared."

"Hell, I'd be, too."

Paul arrived in Becton for a short furlough before being shipped to Vietnam. He tried several times to reach Irene but couldn't. "Damn, where the hell is she? Why doesn't she call me?"

Chapter 21

Paul's plane stopped in San Francisco for a brief layover on the way to Vietnam. He went to a phone booth and called Irene. No answer.

"Damn, I gotta talk to her because I won't be back for twenty months, if I make it back at all."

Some twenty-two hours later, Paul's infantry division landed in Bin Boa, Vietnam, around four o'clock in the afternoon on a very, very hot day. He looked around at his new life of seeing helicopters, tanks, warplanes, and other equipment of war. As they were being driven to their barracks, Paul saw a truck of full body bags. A cold sweat seeped from his pores. Death was all around him.

"Listen up!" the first sergeant shouted. "Welcome to Vietnam. Your army unit is the Fifth Air Calvary, and don't ever forget it. You've already received orientation on the flight over, but I want to emphasize a few things. This is unlike any experience you've had in your lives. It's going to make you scared, physically sick, angry, apprehensive, homesick and some of you, addicted to drugs. Drugs are plentiful in this country."

A soldier standing next to Paul started a casual conversation to anyone within earshot who would listen.

"You know I heard that guys have been killed or wounded on their first day in Vietnam or on their last day of service when they're getting ready to come home. You know, they say that being point man, radio man, or a man carrying automated weapons is the worst position to be in. Guys were breaking their wrist and other things just to get out of the battle zone."

"Okay, okay," the first sergeant said. "Stop running off at the mouth, soldier. If I hear you telling stories like this again, I'll put you on kitchen police for one week and make you do 1,000 pushups. Do I make myself clear?"

"Yes, sir," the soldier said.

"Start pitching tents, and get yourselves organized," the first sergeant said. "I want your rifle cleaned spotlessly because it will be your best friend here in Vietnam. If it jams up because of your negligence to clean it, you won't be able to protect yourself and you're a dead man walking. I'll hold an inspection later today and anyone with a dirty rifle will be looking at sixteen straight hours of guard duty. Do I make myself clear?"

"Yes, sir," everyone shouted.

Paul helped his fellow soldiers set up tents next to the compound. He later grabbed his M1 rifle and sat alone in the front of the compound, cleaning it.

A tall, skinny, bowlegged black soldier stopped in front of Paul. "You look like you know what you're doing," the soldier said.

"Not really. One thing that stuck out in my mind about the orientation is that this rifle is my best friend, so I'm going to try to get it in the best shape possible."

"My name is Bo," the soldier said, extending his hand to shake Paul's.

"Mine is Paul. Good to meet you."

"Where you from, man?"

"Becton, New York. And you?"

"Pittsburgh, Pennsylvania. Were you drafted?"

"Yeah, that's the only way they could get me here. What about you?" Paul asked.

"Same as you, I was drafted. Man, I'm looking to do my time and get the hell out of here." Bo said.

"It looks like we think the same way. What do you think of us being here? Man, I don't know much of why we're in this war, but I did do one thing right after I received my assignment. I went to the library and looked up this place. Do you know this war has been going on since 1954?"

"Say what?" Bo asked.

"Yep. I read some articles to try to get an understanding of why we're fighting this war, but it's way over my head."

"Well, I'll tell you one damn thing. I don't like it because there are too many 'brothers' getting killed over here, and for what? We still have discrimination at home and yet they want us to be patriotic and help the country. Why don't they do something about all that discrimination at home? Like Muhammad Ali said, 'I ain't got no quarrel with them Vietcong. They never called me the N-word.'" Bo said.

Pow! Pow! Pow! Pow! Pow! Paul and Bo dove for the ground and crawled to the corner. Paul's heart thumped out of control. Other soldiers scrambled for cover. There was a deafening silence for two minutes!

"Okay, listen up, listen up!" the first sergeant shouted. "The shots were fired from some distance away. You're going to hear these shots at any time, so take them seriously and prepare to run for cover every time. Continue doing what you were doing."

"Well, this is what we have to look forward to for the next two years. Ducking bullets and being scared half to death. Ain't this a bitch?" Paul snapped.

"We'll make it. Don't worry, we'll make it. Let's go to chow," Bo said.

* * *

It rained almost every day, the heat was intense, and the mosquitoes kept the soldiers company. It was the standard climate in Bin Boa.

Paul became a member of Unit I. His assignment, along with other soldiers, was to help airlift the dead and wounded. It was a gruesome task which Paul despised.

"I hear moaning. Look, over there!" Paul shouted. Paul and a medic rushed the stretcher to the wounded soldier. A soldier lay with shrapnel dug into his thigh and he was losing blood fast. Paul grabbed the soldier by the shoulders and helped lay him on the stretcher. The medic immediately applied a tourniquet to relieve the bleeding.

"Hey, man, you're going to be all right," Paul said. "We're going to get you to the complex and you'll be airlifted for medical attention. Here's some water. Just hang in there, okay?"

The soldier nodded as he lay shaking, in his bloody clothes and one missing boot. "Oh, it hurts so much.

* * *

Paul and his unit pushed farther into the battle zone, looking for dead or wounded soldiers. As they were walking in woods with high grass, they were ambushed.

Pow! Pow! Pow! Everyone stayed low but they were pinned down. Paul looked up and saw his first death – the point man was hit in the chest with a B40 rocket. His body disintegrated!

Paul threw up. He grabbed the medic crouched next to him and shook from head to toe. "Oh, man! Oh, man!" Paul cried.

"Everyone, stay down," the platoon leader ordered.

Paul lay snug to the ground. He threw up again and felt like crying, but he focused on being a soldier. No time for crying now. The shots stopped and then started again.

The platoon leader directed a soldier to send up smoke fifty or one hundred feet in front of their position. The strategy included alerting the Cobra helicopters to attack Vietcong gunfire in front of the smoke signals.

The helicopters cleared the Vietcong from the area but Paul and his crew couldn't get to the wounded and dead for hours for fear of another ambush.

When the gunfire stopped, Paul and the medics rushed to the wounded and assisted those who were still alive. Then they performed the grisly task of putting the dead into body bags. He shook feverishly. The task gagged him and gave him severe headaches. He continued to collect dog tags from the dead for identification.

The platoon leader yelled, "Do we have all the wounded and dead?"

"Yeah," Paul said as he and other soldiers bagged and loaded the last dead soldier on the stretcher.

"Okay, let's move out!"

* * *

Because of their success and efficiency, top officers reassigned Paul's unit to help the marines with the TET (New Year) Offensive. The North Vietnamese regular army and the Vietcong launched this invasion by attacking Saigon, an American outpost at Khe Sahn and the U.S. Embassy compound.

U.S. casualties peaked to 5,000 in three months. Paul's unit lost many soldiers and several were fearful of the war's outcome, including Paul.

He approached his first sergeant at morning breakfast about the recent spate of killings.

"Sergeant Phillips, I'm concerned about the recent invasion on U.S. facilities and the increase in killings of soldiers and marines. I know I'm just a private, but can I ask you a question?

"Sure."

"Are we winning this damn war?"

The sergeant's head moved backward. His eyes widened, and he licked his lips. He took a deep breath and then exhaled slowly. He moved his chair closer to the table and leaned over.

"Private Hodge, what kind of dumb, jack-ass question is that to ask me? Do you want me to call General William Westmoreland and personally ask him if we're winning the war? Look, at my level they don't tell me shit. My job is to keep up the unit's morale and follow orders."

"Okay, Okay, I didn't mean to piss you off."

"I'm sorry, kid. I've got twenty-five years of military service and I want to tell you a secret because I like you. You seem like a kid that I can trust but you have to keep this between us."

Paul nodded, and then said "Yes, I'll keep it a secret." He got closer to the table to listen to the sergeant.

"I am scared myself because it doesn't look like we're winning. You know CBS anchorman Walter Cronkite visited before you reached here. He wrote a report which said that we are stuck in a war that is a stalemate.

You know what that means, don't you? It means, if the public hears about his report, Americans will not support this war. We're not winning and we sure as hell are losing soldiers left and right. Why are we still here? I don't like it, but I can't do anything about it."

Paul stared at Sergeant Phillips. He shook his head.

"I have that feeling, too. I have an even stronger feeling that we're losing the war. But thanks for being honest with me. You took a chance by sharing your feelings, but you can count on me to keep this between us. I am a man of my word."

* * *

During the next six months, Paul was involved in numerous battles where he continued to witness the death of many of his comrades and enemies. Paul's new job was to man the M60 general purpose machine gun. The action was close and furious. He killed several Vietcong soldiers during that time, and was promoted to corporal.

But he felt different inside.

"Hey, Paul," a soldier shouted as they passed through the chow line. "You leave a chick at home?"

Paul glared at the soldier and responded, "What's it to you?"

"Just asking, cuz. All of us here are going to have to work extra hard to get back our chicks we left home. Some 'Jody' got a head start on us and is beating our time."

Paul picked up a small glass of milk and continued to walk slowly through the chow line, looking at the hot food ahead. "Look, speak for yourself, buddy."

"Oh, like it isn't happening to you! We're all being two-timed by some chick back home so don't act like it's not happening to you, too. Just don't let your imagination run away about what he's doing with your chick." The soldier stared at Paul, then cracked a sneaky smile and gave the "v" sign.

Paul abruptly left his food tray on the railing, cut across the line and grabbed the soldier by his collar, lifting him so high that his toes were suspended in air.

"Look, turkey, what's your problem? I ain't taking no shit from you or anyone else. So keep your comments to yourself or we can go outside with this."

"Okay, man, I was just messing with you. Hell, I asked a couple of guys the same question earlier and they just laughed about it. Man, I didn't think you would react like that."

Paul got back in line, picked up the remainder of his meal, and went to the far corner of the mess hall to eat by himself.

Something is coming over me, Paul thought. I got this anger issue and I feel like challenging everyone. I've got to see a doctor.

* * *

"Corporal Hodge, you have a strong case of situational disorder," the post doctor concluded. "Can you tell me what you're feeling now?"

"I'm feeling damn mad because we don't belong here fighting these people. Why are we here? Can you tell me? I also have flashbacks of the killings I've witnessed and it's making me sick."

"I see," the doctor said. "You're not going to agree with me, but you're one of the lucky ones."

"What? I'm all messed up and I'm one of the lucky ones? What do you mean?"

"Many of the other soldiers have lost their limbs, eyesight, arms, and will find it difficult to function once they process back into society. So, consider yourself very fortunate. I want you to take these pills until you leave here, then sign up for regular visits with a doctor at a local Veterans Hospital when you go stateside. If you do exactly what the doctor says, you will be fine."

The doctor's analysis somewhat lightened his concerns. He believed now that he might very well be one of the fortunate ones.

"Thanks, sir. I certainly feel better about this. How long will I have to go to a shrink?"

"I wouldn't call them 'shrinks.' Their goal is to help you rid yourself of the anger you have. The flashbacks you are experiencing will gradually go away as long as you continue following the doctor's instructions."

"Okay, sir, I probably won't see you before I ship out. Thanks for everything and I apologize for giving you a hard time."

"No need to apologize. You're a strong and intelligent young man. You'll get through this. Oh, one other thing. Be sure you file a claim with the Veterans Administration about your condition. You may be eligible to receive monthly financial payments for life."

Chapter 22

As President Richard M. Nixon took office in 1969, the American death toll in the Vietnam War reached over 34,000. The American public grew weary of the war and demanded that the U.S. get out, now.

By January, 1970, even more opposition to the war was evident. Paul went to the Post Exchange and bought a newspaper. He hadn't read any newspapers since arriving in Vietnam. The special edition newspaper contained highlights of year 1969:

- Veteran's Day ceremonies around the country consisted of pro-American demonstrations. An estimated 250,000 people marched on Washington, D.C. to protest the war, while 100,000 marched simultaneously in San Francisco;
- The U.S. won the space race convincingly by landing a man on the moon. Neil Armstrong, Edwin Aldrin, and Michael Collins flew aboard Apollo 11;
- Charles Manson and several members of his cult were charged with the brutal murders of actress Sharon Tate and five others in Los Angeles, the crime, referred to as "Helter Skelter;"
- Senator Ted Kennedy drove his car off a bridge on Chappaquiddick Island, Martha's Vineyard, killing his young passenger, Mary Jo Kopechne. Kennedy received a suspended sentence;

- Recording of the year – "Aquarius/Let the Sunshine In;"
- Album of the Year-*Blood, Sweat and Tears;*
- Best Picture – *Midnight Cowboy*; and
- Movie star Judy Garland died of a drug overdose at age forty-seven.

"Man, there's a lot going on at home that I didn't have a clue about. I'm ready to get out of this damn place and go home where I really can be a part of society. There's nothing here for me but a bullet with my name on it," Paul said with his head down.

"Hey, Corporal. Where are you supposed to be?" Sergeant Phillips asked with a smirk.

"Oh, hi, Sergeant Phillips. Are you serious?"

"No, just messing with you. You're getting to be a short timer, aren't you?"

"Yeah, I got thirty-one days left in this mess."

"Oh, you got it down to the amount of days, do you?"

"You bet. That's how much I want out of this place. Did you see the newspaper?"

"No, what's going on?"

"Remember that serious discussion we had last year about this war? Well read this," Paul said, pointing to the uproar and protest marching.

Sergeant Phillips read it and nodded. "Yep, that CBS news anchor's assessment of the war got out to the public and now the public is outraged. This war will be history in about two years, you mark my word."

"I sure hope so – it's gone on way too long. I just feel sorry for the families that have lost loved ones or who have seriously wounded family members as a result of this war. What do they have to show for it? Nothing!"

"What about you, Sergeant Phillips? You don't seem to be too much into this war. You're in a position of authority where you must carry out orders. How does this make you feel now that you know public outrage is mounting fast?" Paul asked.

"Terrible! Terrible! But I can't show it because I have a job to do and my men depend on me to lead the way."

"Lead the way to what, to *victory?*" Look, we're losing this war! We're losing this war and the American public knows it. When the troops find out that the American public does not support this war, there are going to be some serious morale problems, and that's going to affect your ability to 'lead.' The troops are going to want to come home and there will be many, many AWOL cases. I'm not trying to be a smartass about this; it's just common sense."

"Don't worry, Corporal Hodge. I've also been thinking over the past year. I'm sort of a career soldier because I re-enlisted four times. I'm not married, so I'm not worried about having to support a family. Therefore, I decided this will be my last term in the army. I have eighteen months to go and that's it. I hope to retrain as a civilian and find a decent job. So you see, although I'm older than you, we kind of see eye to eye. This war weighs heavily on your mind because you're intelligent, educated; you questioned the purpose of it from the time you got here. You appear to know what you want to do in life, and, for that, I admire you. You've given me some spark for my future. I'm fortunate that our paths crossed."

Paul smiled and shook Sergeant Phillips' hand.

"Please look me up when you get back in the U.S. My parents in Becton, New York will know how to reach me. Their names are in the telephone book."

"Okay, Corporal Hodge – that's a bet."

* * *

Paul could see Alcatraz as the C-147 carrier plane positioned itself to land. The ancient stone-built ex-prison stood firm with very visible iron bars. The grass looked dead on the little dirt that surrounded the structure. High water splashed off the jagged rocks. He could see the seals and their pups lying on the rocks, sunning. Looking out into the San Francisco Bay, Paul could see the rough waters rocking the small vessels as they passed each other, and the assortment of birds. The Golden Gate Bridge was to his left. It almost seemed like he could reach out and touch it as the plane made its final turn before landing.

Thump! Thump! What the hell was that? It was just the landing wheels coming down. A few seconds went by and then . . . . Boom! Boom! The plane landed roughly as Paul looked at the ground. It moved slower and slower, and finally stopped!

Paul slumped down into his seat and let out a big sigh of relief. He was back in the "world." Safely! He continued to sit for a few minutes as the other soldiers filed out of the plane, shaking each other's hands and patting each other on the backs.

"Congratulations, man," a voice said from behind Paul.

Paul turned around and it was a smiling soldier, leaning on a crutch, a person he had seen before in the complex but did not know.

"Hey, man, thanks, and congratulations to you as well," Paul said as he shook the soldier's hand. Paul allowed him to go ahead of him to the exit and patted him on the shoulders.

* * *

Paul arrived at John F. Kennedy Airport and took a bus to Becton, where he hailed a cab.

"Where you going, son?" the cab driver asked.

"Take me to 285 Summit Street."

"Are you from here?"

"Yes."

"Where are you coming from?

Paul hesitated. "Vietnam."

"Oh, man, you've been there? What do you think about the war now that you've been there?"

"Look, I don't want to talk about it. Just take me to the address that I gave you."

The cab driver looked in the rear mirror at Paul and adjusted it so Paul was out of his view. He said nothing the rest of the way.

Paul walked slowly toward the front door. He wondered how he was going to look to his parents. Would they detect his change in character?

Paul's dog, Skippy met him at the door and started barking wildly. Then it growled loudly and pulled violently at his pant leg. "Grrr! Grrr! Grrr!"

"Skippy, it's me," Paul said. "You forgot me, huh, boy?" as he patted Skippy on the head. Skippy started sniffing. The more he sniffed, the less he pulled on Paul's pants. Skippy then began making whimpering sounds and suddenly, his tail wagging increased. Skippy then jumped madly up and down, probably fifty times.

The door opened and Paul's parents ran to him with hugs and kisses. Paul tried to be as normal as possible.

"Welcome home, son," Mr. Hodge said.

"I'm glad to be home. You don't know how glad I am to be home," Paul said with a wide grin.

Paul's parents walked into the house with their arms around their son.

"I know you're hungry, Paul. I just fixed dinner." his mother said.

"I'm starving for your cooking, Mom, so don't be light on the portions." Paul quickly devoured the crock-pot cooked turkey wings, rice, and carrots like a starving, homeless person. He topped that off with a slice of carrot cake and a cup of coffee. He smiled at his mom and said, "Military food never tasted this good. You're the best."

Paul's mother just smiled.

"Well, son, what was it like over . . . ?" Paul's father asked.

"Dad, I don't want to talk about it, now, or ever."

Paul's father was taken aback by Paul's snappy response. He dropped the newspaper and his mouth flew open. "What happened out there, son?" Paul's father asked again, leaning forward in his chair.

Paul's mother stepped in. "Now, George, Paul must be tired after such a long trip. Let's give him some space and privacy and let him get some rest."

"Sorry, son, I didn't mean to meddle," Paul's father said.

"That's okay, Dad." Paul excused himself from the table and went to his room. It hadn't been disturbed after nearly two years and still contained his track trophies, high school and college diplomas, and other familiar items.

The items comforted him. He sat on the bed and thought about his future – graduate school, get out of Becton, and find a good-paying job in a big city.

Chapter 23

"Mom and Dad, Howard University accepted me for its graduate program."

"Great, son," his father said. "I am so proud of you. I'm going to help you financially because I know it's expensive."

"Thanks, Dad, I really appreciate that. The army will pay for some of the courses under the G.I. Bill, but anything you can contribute will help."

"Son, you've been through a lot. Keep making us proud," his mother said, pinching Paul on the cheek.

"Okay, I gotta call Oscar and tell him the good news."

* * *

"Hey, Oscar, I'm back in town."

"Man, it's good to hear your voice. Is everything okay?"

"Yeah, man, everything's fine. I've already made plans to get out of Becton. I'm going to Washington, D.C."

"Hey, man, what's happening there?"

"Graduate school at Howard University."

"You've been accepted?"

"Yep."

"Oh, man, that's great news. Are you going to study or chase those pretty girls?"

"I'm gonna do both," Paul said as he chuckled over the telephone receiver. "Man, I'm excited. D.C. is a good employment center for professionals so it shouldn't be hard to find a job after I graduate. Are you coming down to see me, man?"

"Hell, yeah. I hear the city has a large black population and they party seven days a week. The comparison to Becton is like day and night. Man, I envy you."

"You want to go to the movies tonight to see *The Towering Inferno*? A lot of stars are playing in it, like Robert Wagner, Fred Astaire, Fay Dunaway, Steve McQueen, O.J. Simpson, and others."

"Yeah, man, let's go."

Paul picked up Oscar an hour later and headed to the movies. As he pulled into the movie parking lot, his favorite station played "Killing Me Softly With His Song" by Roberta Flack. Paul turned off the motor, then turned the radio back on without starting the car. As Oscar was about to exit the car, Paul said, "Hold it. I've got to hear the rest of this song. This is a bad song." Oscar closed the door, leaned back and listened to the song, too.

"Man, I wish you could turn into Irene. That song has me going."

"I can't help you there, man. Have you told Irene about your acceptance to graduate school?"

"Not yet. I'll call her."

* * *

"Hi, is this the Veterans Hospital?" Paul asked.

"Yes, it is. Can I help you?" the male voice asked.

"I'd like to set up an appointment with a doctor that handles situational disorders – or stress response syndrome. I recently returned from Vietnam and my unit doctor asked me to follow up at a Veterans Hospital about my condition."

"Okay, you're calling the right number. Fridays are the days we see patients with your concerns. Just walk in from 9 a.m. to 4 p.m., and one of our doctors will see you."

Paul walked into the hospital, signed in. He waited only a few minutes before being called.

"Paul Hodge?" the doctor said.

Paul went with the doctor to the examination room.

The doctor, a middle-aged man with a slight mustache, smiled at Paul. "My name is Dr. Gadek." He extended his hand to shake Paul's. "Did you bring your military medical records with you?"

"Yes, sir."

"I want to take a few minutes to review your records. Feel free to read some books or change the channels on the TV. I'll be back in a few minutes."

Dr. Gadek returned. "I've reviewed your records, and, based on my observation of you, plus our brief conversation, I believe that you're a lucky young man."

Paul sat mute.

"Before we start, I must ask you a question. Did you get involved in any drug usage like marijuana, opium, or heroin while in Vietnam?"

"Absolutely not."

"Good. I am happy with your response because, if you had, it would have a negative effect on your condition and recovery period. Paul, what you have is very treatable, and, with a little medication, you should be fine. All you have to do is manage your anger and anxiety, continue to improve your communication skills, use relaxation techniques, and I can provide you with some information about the relationship between your thoughts and feelings. During your periodic visits, I will continue to talk to you about the trauma you suffered and the negative feelings associated with the events of your experience in Vietnam."

Paul said, "Phew, I'm glad my condition is treatable. Thank you, thank you so much. You've taken a load off of mind."

"Paul, I want you to be happy, but I must be truthful. Treating your condition may take a long, long time, and even then you may not be totally cured. I just want you to know the truth."

"Well, I appreciate your honesty, Doctor."

Chapter 24

Paul called Irene the next day to share his new fortune.

"Hi, what's happening?"

"Nothing much," Irene responded.

"Guess what? I've been accepted for graduate school at Howard University in D.C."

"Oh, that's fabulous news. When did you find out?"

"Last week."

"It looks like we're going to be separated, again. I guess we've got to sacrifice something in order to prepare for our working life."

"Yeah, but we'll be all right."

"There's going to be a large demonstration in Washington, D.C. next month, protesting the Vietnam War. I'm planning to go because too many of our boys are being killed and we are not winning the war. The big protest is scheduled for May 3rd, and it's called May Day Protests."

"I see you've been following the events of the war?"

"Yes. Would you like to go with me?

"Oh, I'd love to go."

* * *

Cars poured into D.C. from everywhere, causing massive traffic jams. Anti-war activists called for shutting down the federal government, and Paul and Irene were right in the mix of things.

"Who's actually leading this demonstration?" Paul asked.

Irene, holding Paul's hand and looking all around at the massive gathering, said, "I hear it's a group called the Mayday Tribe. I don't know anything about them, but I hear they're very aggressive."

"Okay!" A guy with a large handlebar mustache bellowed into a large bull horn. "Our goal is to shut down the government and create so much chaos that the only way the political leaders could end the chaos would be to stop the war. We're going to have small groups block major intersections and bridges into the Capitol and roads into the city. Remember: This is a nonviolent demonstration, but protect yourselves where necessary."

"Move on, move on," a policeman said, poking Paul in his ribs with a night stick.

Paul yelled, "Hey, man, you don't have to use that stick, I'm moving."

"I said, *move!*"

"I'm moving, but don't touch me with that stick again or you're going to have problems."

Irene grabbed Paul by the arm and hustled him away from the policeman.

"You can't get into a confrontation with these policemen. They're looking for some heads to crack. Cool it, Paul."

The crowds kept coming. Reinforcements in the form of federal troops numbering 10,000 besieged D.C. It was getting crazy.

"Stay close to me, Irene, because it's getting too dangerous to be out here. Do you smell that? They're using tear gas. Look, they're arresting a lot of people. Give me your hand."

Paul and Irene scampered from the area where the police sprayed tear gas. They sat on the well-manicured grass away from the crowd in Potomac Park. The Thomas Jefferson Memorial and paddle boats made an interesting background.

Paul turned on his small white Motorola radio to listen to the media coverage of the protest. Shock waves passed through his body as he held the radio close to his ears.

"This is your noontime WCCB AM news. The anti-war protest in Washington, D.C. is at full throttle. More than 10,000 people have been arrested, making it the largest mass arrest in U.S. history. That number is continuing to rise. This protest is several days old, with the federal troopers and National Guard, along with local police, fortunately having gained control of the disorder. The reported problems were initiated by two factions: The Mayday Tribe and the Yippies. They disrupted traffic and caused chaos in the streets. Authorities arrested many innocent citizens. There are reports that federal employees were held hostage in their offices. Our recommendation is not to come to this area of the city because it could blow up at any time. We will interrupt programming on this station to give hourly updates."

Paul grabbed both of Irene's hands and looked directly into her eyes. "This is getting to be a dangerous scene. We certainly can't afford to get arrested because we're both going to graduate school. Our bridge to a successful future is right around the corner. Our minds and bodies must be in great shape. Everything must be perfect in order to tackle the difficult subjects we've chosen. Do you get where I'm going?"

"Yes, I do, and I totally agree with you. I think we've done our share to show that we are against continuation of the war. Our presence is supportive enough. Let's blow this joint."

"Yeah, let's go."

* * *

Paul and Irene drove to a public park just outside of Becton. The May breezes blew the honeysuckle fragrance past their noses and put them in a sentimental mood.

Paul said, "Well, I guess we won't be seeing each other for a while. You'll still mean the most to me and I know you feel the same about me. We've been away from each other before, so it won't be too hard this time. What are you feeling?"

Silence.

"I'm scared. I'm sort of split between my desire to go back to school and being separated from you again." She sniffled. "I know that we've got to prepare for our careers, but it's difficult not seeing you for long periods of time. Will you always think about me?"

"Oh, most definitely. Do you remember that promise we made to each other about always seeing each other? Well, it's still sizzling and for real. We're both for real – we haven't changed and we're not going to change."

Silence.

Paul finally said, "This is a big test for both of us. Let's see if we both can stand up to the challenge. Okay?"

"Okay."

"Meanwhile, are you ready to have our last rendezvous for a while?"

"I can't wait."

Chapter 25

As Paul approached his car, he held his arms up high and screamed, "Yes! Yes! Yes! Look out, D.C., here I come!"

Paul's Dad purchased a car for his trip to D.C. He told his friends good-bye and headed down Interstate 95 South to Howard University in Washington, D.C.

The six-hour drive gave him time to think and to anticipate. He knew there was something missing from the excitement of his new life in a new city. Irene Dudash!

As Paul walked down Georgia Avenue toward Crampton Auditorium for orientation, a voice yelled, "Go Shaw, Go Shaw, Go Shaw." Paul looked around and saw his old college friend, Al Roundtree.

"What the hell are you doing here?" Paul asked with a wide grin, shaking Al's hand.

"I'm taking graduate classes in hospital administration," Al responded. "What about you?"

"I'm pursuing my MBA. This is my first year."

"Well, I'm happy as hell you're here. You know how lonesome it gets on campus when you don't know anyone," Al said.

"Yeah, I know what you mean. Hey look, I hear there's a watering hole a few blocks up the street called Kenyon Grill. A brother told me the place rocks with chicks. Want to go, sometime?"

"Most definitely. Let's check out our schedules and plan from there."

During the next two weeks, Paul studied hard to get a head start on his courses and strived to adjust to graduate studies. His grades had to be maintained at a "B" level to stay in school. As soon as he felt comfortable enough with his progress, he called Al.

"How are your studies going, Al?"

"Not as well as I would like, but I need a break. I think I'm trying too hard. What's happening?

"Let's go to the Kenyon Grill and see what's happening. I don't know the city that well but I'll find you. Where do you live?"

"I live in a rooming house on Lincoln Road, Northeast."

Kenyon Grill wasn't an impressive looking place from the outside with its dark green painted doors and dingy windows. But once Paul and Al entered the door – well, that was another story. There were beautiful women everywhere, the males were friendly, and the walls were covered with large black-and-white photos of Muhammad Ali, Josephine Baker, Dr. Martin Luther King, Jr., Malcom X, Lena Horne, Charlie Parker, and other black notables. Above all, the food looked fabulous.

The booths were filled and Paul and Al had to wait for a seat. About ten minutes passed when a fellow asked them, "Hey brothers, do you want this booth – we're leaving."

"Thanks," Paul said.

As soon as they sat down, a beautiful young lady walked up to the juke box, smiling at Paul as she passed his booth. Her naturally smooth and teasing tan complexion caught Paul's eye. Physically she was well-endowed, her ponytail wagged from side to side when she walked, and her ultra-white teeth sparkled when she smiled. She played several songs. Among them were "Let's Do It Again," by the Staples Singers; "Boogie on Reggae Woman," by Stevie Wonder; "What Am I Going To Do With You?," by Barry White, and a new hit song and dance style, "The Hustle," by Van McCoy.

After the songs stopped playing, Paul walked over to the young lady who selected the songs and said, "Hi, my name is Paul. You have good musical taste. I liked every one of your selections."

"Hi, my name is Terri Rogers. I'm happy to meet you, Paul. These are my friends, Tempura, and Phillissa."

"Hi ladies, it's nice to meet you both. Terri, I hate to ask this question because I know it sounds so phony, but do you come here often?" Paul asked in a whispering voice.

"Yes, quite often. I like the atmosphere and the people are friendly."

"This is my first time here and I like it. I know I'll be returning." Paul flashed a broad smile. "I just started graduate school so I'll be around."

"I'm in my junior year majoring in business administration."

"Oh, that's great. I'm studying for my MBA. Please let me know if you need any assistance." Paul wrote down his number and gave it to Terri. He walked back to his booth and said to himself, damn, she's fine.

"Man, she's a choice chick. How you gonna study and try and get next to that, too?" Al asked.

"Oh, don't worry, I'll find a way."

* * *

"Hello, may I speak to Paul?"

"This is Paul."

"Paul, this is Terri. I met you at the Kenyon Grill a few weeks ago."

"Hi Terri, how have you been?"

"Good. I wanted to take you up on your offer of assistance with my accounting. Are you busy?

"No, not at all. Are you having problems?"

"Somewhat. I don't have a good grasp on an accounting issue. I'm sort of stuck on closing the accounts of proprietorships, partnerships, and corporations."

"I can help you with that. Do you want me to come over?"

"Well, I have a roommate and she's got company. Would it be asking too much for you to pick me up and go to your place?"

"Absolutely not.

Paul threw his arms in the air and closed his fists after hanging up the phone. He couldn't believe Terri had called him and his heart pumped rapidly. He ran to the bedroom to get clean underwear, he ran to the bathroom to run the shower, then back to the bedroom, slipped and fell on the bedroom rug, then to the bathroom, all in a wild frenzy.

Paul knocked on the door and waited for it to open. The lock turned and Terri stood in the doorway. She wore a pink, short-sleeved blouse, a pair of Liz Claiborne jeans, and brown Bass Weejun loafers with white socks.

"Come in, Paul, I'll be ready in a jiffy. Oh, this is my roommate, Veronica, and her friend, Devin."

"I'm pleased to meet you." Paul looked around the apartment and focused on a photo sitting on the coffee table of Terri and her parents. He smiled.

"Okay, Paul, I'm ready. See you guys later."

Paul headed west and wondered how the night would turn out.

They entered Paul's apartment, which he cleaned thoroughly before he left to pick up Terri. Everything was placed in an orderly fashion. The parquet floors gleamed, the pillows on the sofa were strategically placed, and a photograph of his parents sat on a glass counter.

"We can sit over here," Paul said, pointing to a small mahogany wooden table. Paul pulled up two chairs and Terri pulled out her accounting book. She explained where she was having difficulty.

Paul listened intently, and then responded, "In the section you are dealing with, the work sheet in accounting procedures is most important. Just remember that a work sheet has five columns: trial balance, adjustments, adjusted trial balance, income statement, and balance sheet. We can go over this so you'll understand the process."

Paul and Terri spent two hours discussing Terri's accounting class. "Thank you for your help. I understand the assignment better now," Terri said.

"Are you sure?"

"Yes."

"Okay, can I get you something to drink?"

"Just water, please."

Paul returned with a glass of water, gave it to Terri, and turned on the radio. "Cruisin" by Smokey Robinson played on WUST, a local station which Paul found to his liking. It reminded him of his beloved WNJR.

"Do you keep up with music and artists?" Paul asked.

"I know some of the songs, but unless it's a hit I'm afraid I'm not that good with names. What about you?"

"Oh, this is my thing. I follow the music and artists closely. Been doing it all my life, so it's just something I do well. Would you like to dance?"

"Sure."

Paul and Terri slow-danced to Smokey's hit song, and then continued dancing to Lou Rawls's "You'll Never Find Another Love Like Mine."

"I've got to get up early tomorrow so I guess I should go," Terri said.

"Yeah, it is getting late. I hope I've been helpful."

"You have, and thank you so much."

"I'd like to see you again, soon, very soon."

"I'd like that, Paul. Just call me."

* * *

Paul's parents forwarded to him a Christmas card which Irene had sent him.

It was his only contact with her in over a year. No calls were initiated by either one before or after Paul received the card.

The card read:

"Good hope, Good will, Good friends –

Wishing you joy that never ends.

Always. Irene."

Paul held the card in his hand and looked at the floor. "Well, I haven't heard from her so I guess both of us compromised our promise to always see each other. Well, I know why I haven't contacted her. Terri! Yeah, I have some strong feelings for Terri and I don't need the hassle of worrying about Irene. She may have someone else, herself."

* * *

Paul and Terri dated for two years. He eventually completed graduate school and she received her BA degree.

"Hey Terri, meet me at the Kenyon Grill at about three o'clock."

"Okay, see you then."

Paul arrived early, hoping that he could beat the late afternoon crowd. Lunch time customers had gone. He sat at a booth but placed his hat and coat across from him as though someone were already sitting there. He wanted no company this day.

He saw Terri arrive and waved his hands frantically. She walked briskly to the booth.

"Hi baby, I see you're on time and I like that," Paul said.

"I try."

Paul called the waitress over. "Hi, can I have a bottle of champagne? I want it super cold and on ice."

"Yes, sir, coming right up."

"Paul, are we celebrating something?"

"We will be."

The waitress brought the champagne and placed it beside Paul. He didn't take his gaze off of Terri while he shined up the glasses with his pure white napkin. He took a deep breath and held Terri's hands across the table.

"I have one statement to make and one question to ask. I want to celebrate both."

"Go right ahead, you have the floor." Terri said.

Paul squeezed Terri's hands and stared into her eyes. "I've been selected for a job here in Washington, D.C. and I've accepted it."

"That's great. What kind of job is it?"

"I've been hired as a management trainee with Bartlett Foods Corporation. When I complete my training, I'll be working in personnel, operations, and sales and marketing."

"I'm so happy for you, Paul."

Paul licked his dry lips and continued the conversation. "You blew my mind the first time I laid eyes on you. Those feelings haven't let up one bit. Well, now that I've got a job, which eventually will be paying good money, I want to settle down, but I need a mate. I want us spend our future together. Will you marry me?"

Terri jerked her hands away from Paul's grasp and placed them over her mouth. Her eyes moistened and soon tears streamed down her cheeks. Her hands shook as she rejoined Paul's hands in union.

"Yes, Paul, yes."

Paul smiled. He grabbed the champagne bottle, popped the cork, filled the glasses, and placed the bottle back in the ice bucket. They sipped champagne, then kissed for several minutes.

Paul and Terri married a few months later and settled in Washington, D.C. They started a family and their daughter, Crystal, was born one year later.

Chapter 26

Irene finished unpacking her bags from the long trip from Becton. Exhaustion consumed her. She sat on the couch and looked over her course schedule. "Wow, Stanford's graduate program is very demanding. I've got to get ahead of the curve on these subjects. I better not contact Paul for a while because I need to concentrate on my studies."

After taking a short nap, Irene headed to Walgreens. She picked up the *Palo Alto Daily News*. The headlines read: "U.S. Withdraws from Vietnam."

"Man, that's great news. Paul and I were a part of history – we helped pressure the U.S. Government to get out of that place." She read further: "In accordance with the Paris Peace Treaty, the U.S., North and South Vietnam, and the Provisional Revolutionary Government, signed an agreement to withdraw their troops."

Another sub-headline caught her eye: "Burglars Are Caught Breaking into Democratic Party Headquarters at Watergate Complex in Washington, D.C."

"What is going on with our politicians? This is going to be a mess when it's all straightened out, if at all."

Irene drove back to the dormitory. She turned on the radio, searching for a station that played her type of music. Bingo! KZSU 90.1 AM played

"Neither One of Us," by Gladys Knight and the Pips, "That Lady," by the Isley Brothers, and "Ain't No Woman (Like The One I've Got)," by the Four Tops.

"Wow! If I use this station for company while here at Stanford, I'm going to make it through school all right."

* * *

A year passed, and Irene did well with her studies. On the way to the grocery store one day, a voice behind her said, "Can I have a word with you?"

Irene turned around but kept walking. The strapping guy approached, caught up to her, and repeated, "Can I have a word with you?"

Irene stopped.

"My name is Jeremy." He stood six feet four inches tall, with dirty-blond hair. His trim body belied his 230 pounds, and his good-natured demeanor blended well with Irene's.

"My name is Irene."

"Irene, please forgive my awkwardness, but I've been seeing you around campus for several months and I just had to know your name."

"Well, now you know it. What program are you in?"

"Engineering. And you?"

"Ed.M program."

"That's great. I know that you have a tough study schedule but I'd like to take you to lunch when you have a break. Is that possible?"

"Sure, why not? Say, do you play football?"

"I did, right here. I got hurt in my senior year and that was it. I never had professional football aspirations, and always planned to get my engineering degree. Can I call you?"

"Sure." Irene gave Jeremy her number.

* * *

Irene became good friends with a young lady named Pat, with whom she took classes. They lived in the same apartment complex.

Pat knocked on Irene's door one evening. "Hi, are you busy?"

"I am, but I need a break. Please come in. Here, let me move some of these books and papers so you can sit down."

"Oh, thanks. How are your studies going?" Pat asked.

"They're coming along well, thank you. My goals and objectives are to get ahead of the curve, not fall behind. As you know, once you fall behind, pressure to do well and complete the assignments in a timely manner begins to build. I don't like pressure. How about you?"

"I'm also doing well. There's not much to do in this area, so I focus on my studies. By the way, what do you plan to do when you graduate?"

"Probably too much," Irene said as she nodded. She took a deep breath and exhaled. "I've narrowed it down to working with disadvantaged kids, either through the public education system or private groups. I'm leaning toward living in Chicago. They have a lot of public-education issues there."

Pat smiled. "I think that's great. Me, after I graduate, I'll probably head back to my small hometown, Deer Lodge, Montana. I'm not a big-city person – the quiet West is good enough for me. I have a job lined up in the education field in Butte. I also plan to help my parents raise horses on our farm. I enjoy playing with them, especially the colts. They bring me so much joy."

Irene glanced out the window and with a quizzical look asked, "Say, do you know a guy named Jeremy? I don't know his last name, but he's in the school of engineering program. He's well-built, good-looking, and aggressive."

"You must mean Jeremy Covington. Yes, I know him. He's really a nice guy," Pat said.

"Okay, thanks for the information."

* * *

Jeremy called Irene, and they dated for the remainder of their time at Stanford.

Irene wanted to get away from her grueling studies. She headed east toward the San Francisco Bay area to see the sights. The radio station already was tuned to 90.1. Out came the sounds of, "Bennie and the

Jets," by Elton John, "Boogie Down," by Eddie Kendricks, and "Dancing Machine," by The Jackson 5. They soothed her soul.

The disk jockey interrupted programming: "Richard Nixon has resigned as President of the United States and Gerald Ford has been sworn in as President."

"Wow! I'll be able to tell my kids and grandkids that I lived through some of the most turbulent and time-changing moments in the history of this country."

Irene thought about Paul several times, but never called him.

* * *

Irene graduated from college with honors and stayed in California, doing consulting work in education. Jeremy had also graduated, and they married soon after.

"Hey toots, I got a job offer from Parsons Engineering, Inc., a reputable national company in Chicago. Why don't you apply for a teaching position in the Chicago Public School system so we can live and work in the same city? What do you think?"

"Congratulations on your offer. You're not going to believe this, but that is exactly what I had planned to do. I've already called CPS personnel department for an application. Now, there is something I must discuss with you, and, if you don't mind, I'd like to do it now."

"Sure, go ahead."

"When I apply for a teaching position in Chicago, I'm going to specify that I want to teach in Ward 27. Ward 27 is one of the most notorious in Chicago in that many of the black kids that attend school come from the infamous Cabrini-Green housing projects. I read a series of articles about the area in the newspaper last year, and decided to initiate my teaching career there. They are voiceless people who need education and assistance. Needless to say, there are many dropouts and an increasing crime rate."

Jeremy's mouth flew open, wrinkles appeared on his forehead, and he bowed his head. Silence. He raised his head, shook it, and uttered one word: "Why?"

"I want to try to make a difference in their lives through education. There is no one else fending for them – they are powerless and lack the means to attain economic parity. I want you to understand that this is my calling in life – to help others less fortunate than me."

Jeremy abruptly pushed himself away from the table – his chair squealing – stood up, and walked around the room in circles. After a moment, he spoke with a firm voice.

"But you can do that in other ways. You can donate money to organizations that support blacks or volunteer your time to implement programs, attend civil rights marches to improve their plight in society, and lobby Congress and local elected officials to pass bills to improve schools. Those are tangible ways in which you can get involved. You don't have to put yourself at risk every day as an educator in that environment."

"These kids need to be touched by a caring person at the earliest ages of their lives. It's too late when they get to senior high school. All those things you mentioned are doable and commendable, but I need to be at the grass-roots level so I can be effective. Jeremy, I really need your support."

Jeremy returned to his seat and looked around, trying to find the right words to respond. He placed his right hand under his chin, resembling world-famous French sculptor, Auguste Rodin's, "The Thinker." He responded slowly and deliberately.

"I'm going to be perfectly honest with you. I don't like your plans, but I respect what is in your heart. You're a good person and I know, when you go after something it's hard to turn you around. So let's play it by ear but – oh, all right. I can see you're not going to change your mind."

Irene grinned and placed a kiss on Jeremy's lips.

"Thanks for understanding."

CPS hired Irene almost immediately. Irene and Jeremy headed to Chicago to begin new careers.

After working for three years, Irene took a leave of absence from her school work, returned to Stanford University, and earned a Ph.D in education.

Chapter 27

Paul headed up U.S. Interstate 95 for his long, six-hour drive to Becton and the reunion. He brought along his favorite CDs to keep him company. As he entered the Baltimore-Washington Parkway, he pushed the start button and out came the sounds of Eddie Jefferson, backed up by James Moody and his musicians. Paul loved the 1950's and 1960's jazz musicians. He played it over and over, and, before long, he had crossed the Delaware Memorial Bridge.

Paul played Dakota Staton's "The Late, Late Show" CD several times and several Gloria Lynne CDs, which took him to north Jersey, across the Goethals Bridge. He took the Belt Parkway out of the city and finally reached Becton.

As he was about to ring the doorbell, the door abruptly opened and there stood his aging mother, her face now wrinkled, and hands trembling.

"Hi son, I've been waiting for you for two hours. I kept peeking through the curtains whenever I heard a car door shut." They embraced each other passionately.

"Where's Dad?"

"He's in the bed, sleeping. He hasn't been feeling good, Paul. We've been to the doctor several times but he cannot pinpoint the problem. I guess we're just getting old."

"We all are, Mom. Why don't you and Dad go out for short walks? Maybe that's what he needs, a little exercise."

"I don't think he can do short walks, Paul. It's just our time to get old."

"Just try it, Mom. Look, I've got to get ready for the reunion. I have to be there at six o'clock for cocktail hour. I'm going to run my bath water."

* * *

Paul drove slowly as he entered the hotel parking lot. He saw people exiting cars, but didn't recognize anyone. He looked for his friends, Oscar and Arvin, but didn't see them.

Early arrivals filled the cocktail lounge. Paul nervously walked in and ordered a margarita. As he tipped the waitress, a voice from behind said, "Welcome back to Becton, brother."

Paul abruptly turned around and it was his old friend, Oscar. "Hey man, how you been?" Paul asked as he embraced Oscar with a passionate bear hug.

"I'm holding the down the fort, brother. What about you?"

Paul grabbed Oscar by the arm and both walked to a quiet corner in the cocktail lounge.

"Man, you know I'm on a mission because Irene is supposed to show up. That's the main reason I'm here. If you spot her, let me know. Meanwhile, I'm going to circulate. If they see two brothers quietly talking, they might think something's up." They laughed loudly and separated to greet other classmates.

Several people innocently interrupted his search and engaged in conversation with him. Paul was polite and tried very hard to show interest in the discussions, but his thoughts were on one person only – Irene. His gaze continued to roam during the discussions. He wondered if she looked the same. His scrutiny of the crowd was now in full mode.

Finally, Paul spotted Irene. Bells went off in his head. He started walking sideways through the crowd toward Irene, attempting to make eye contact, simultaneously. And then it happened. A big grin covered Irene's beautiful face. They worked their way toward each other and continued to respectfully shorten their discussions with other classmates.

Several additional minutes passed, and finally they stood in front of each other.

"Irene, you look absolutely great!" Paul said.

Irene returned the compliment. Irene looked splendid in her elegant full-length fuchsia silk dress. She had a long shawl wrapped around her shoulders. Her long, pulled-back graying dark hair resembled the style she wore in high school.

"Can I get you something to drink?" Paul asked.

"White wine will be fine."

Paul ordered another margarita and walked with Irene to a quiet corner. They did not escape the scrutiny of their classmates. Paul periodically looked around and noticed the gazes of several classmates. Paul was much more sensitive to what was going on, but Irene couldn't care less. It was vintage Irene. Paul and Irene continued their long conversation about their lives.

"When did we last see each other?" Irene asked.

"I believe it's been over thirty years."

They focused on each other. They remembered each other as adolescents and young adults, but did not know each other as mature adults.

"Wow! Where has the time gone? How's your family?"

"They're doing fine. What about yours?" Paul asked.

"Thinning out quickly. My mother passed away a few years ago but my father is still living. I married Jeremy whom I met in graduate school, but he passed away nine years ago. I had a daughter, Pamela, who passed away last year from breast cancer. I am able to manage my losses by throwing myself into the lives of my grandsons, Tommy and Teddy. I've raised them since the age of ten years old and now they're nineteen."

Paul froze for a few seconds upon hearing the astonishingly sad news. "I'm so sorry to hear that. I guess we're at a point in our lives where we attend funerals of family and friends more than weddings. That's life!"

"You're right. What about your family?" Irene asked.

"I'm married, and my wife's name is Terri. She's a retail merchandise manager at Macy's. We have one daughter, named Crystal. I retired from Bartlett Foods where I managed domestic and overseas accounts. Now, I spend a lot of time on the Internet, looking for old friends to re-establish treasured relationships."

"That's what I remember about you, the warmness of keeping in touch with people. You've always been a people person. I guess some things never change."

Paul smiled, nodded and said, "I'm going to mingle among the crowd, but I want us to sit together during dinner."

"Okay."

Paul and Irene headed in opposite directions to talk to other classmates.

Thirty minutes passed when the class president grabbed the microphone. "May I have your attention, please? Everyone please find a table so dinner can be served. We'll have a short program after dinner."

Paul looked around for Irene and saw her walking in his direction. They smiled at each other and sat at a front table together, in view of everyone. Paul and Irene had barely scratched the surface with their conversation. Paul desired to continue it throughout the evening, and maybe beyond. He hoped Irene felt the same way.

Four other classmates sat at the table; everyone greeted each other. Paul helped Irene into her seat and pushed her chair closer to the table. Then he took his seat and smiled at Irene.

Paul initiated an almost nonstop conversation, which he sought for years. It was like a dream come true. His conversation with Irene lasted almost four hours. The questions and responses flowed from their mouths like those of a well-prepared law student taking a final oral bar exam.

"I started to say earlier that my daughter, Crystal, is in her second year in college and doing well. And I am proud to say that I live in the greatest and most powerful city in the world, Washington, D.C."

"How in the world did you get to Washington, D.C.?"

"I attended graduate school at Howard University and decided to stay after I got my degree. Remember? I love living there. It's culturally diverse, rich in the arts, with great restaurants, and it's an exciting city where important things happen on a regular basis."

"Sounds like D.C. is your type of city. I've been there a few times. Every year I take a leave of absence from my school position to serve on federal review panels for the American Indian Program Branch, Head Start Bureau.

"Isn't that program under the U.S. Department of Education?"

"Yes, it is. I participate on review panels to try to redirect federal funds to meet the critical needs of Native-Americans to improve the quality of their lives. My passion is to help these people in any way I can."

"Well, for sure you haven't changed from being a sensitive and caring person. Good for you."

Paul and Irene periodically smiled sheepishly, just as they did when they first met in high school.

After dinner the music of the 1960's permeated the air and brought back memories. He hummed along to the familiar music. Romantic songs such as "Love Me All The Way" by Kim Weston, "Gee Whiz" by Carla Thomas, and "In The Still Of The Night" by the Five Satins excited Paul. The music was different from past reunions. This time the DJ was playing Paul's type of music. He extended his hand to dance with Irene.

"May I have this dance?"

Irene smiled, adjusted the shawl on her shoulders, and responded, "Certainly."

Paul helped Irene out of her seat and they headed to the dance floor, hand in hand. They were the only ones on the floor, so their appearance did not go unnoticed. Paul held Irene gently and rocked slowly to the inviting music. Irene laid her head on Paul's broad shoulders, raising it only to hold conversations with Paul.

"This dance is bringing back memories, big time," Paul said.

"Well, it certainly has been a long time since we've done this."

"Yes, it has."

As they danced, others began to join them. The floor became very crowded, and Paul became braver as he continued to dance. Now he was holding Irene closer to his body and she pushed forward, leaving no visible space between them.

When the song ended, Paul and Irene walked back to their seats. Paul, the proverbial gentleman, again helped Irene into her seat and scooted her chair closer to the table.

As Paul casually looked around the banquet room, Irene hit him with a question that shocked him.

"Paul, did anyone tell you that my deceased daughter was bi-racial?"

"No, I didn't know that."

"Yes, she was. She was very brave and demonstrated so much courage during her illness. She was such a battler and I was so proud of her for the comfort she gave me. She taught me a lot about life." Irene took out her wallet and showed Paul her daughter's picture.

"Absolutely beautiful," Paul said.

Irene was fiercely proud of Pamela and spoke with pride of her grandchildren. "Here's a picture of Pamela's twin sons. They're terrific kids and bring joy to my life."

Paul reviewed the pictures carefully, showing keen interest while doing so.

"They're great looking kids. I know they were difficult to raise alone."

"Yes, but Pamela did a great job raising them until her untimely death. She made my job easier."

"It sounds like your daughter was not only an amazing daughter but also an outstanding mother."

The class president started the program. He announced the number of deaths in the class to date, asked for the whereabouts of certain missing classmates, reviewed plans for touring the City of Becton and Becton High School, and went over the time and place for the farewell breakfast, the last item for the reunion weekend.

"Wow, they've really got this reunion together. I think it's good for the classmates who have come from afar to attend – these extra activities will enable us to have more time to talk with each other."

Paul nodded and said, "Yes, I agree."

Minute by minute, Paul and Irene learned more and more about each other as adults. Paul thought Irene was such a beautiful person both inside and outside and that he was blessed to have their friendship renewed after so many years of absence.

The night ended all too quickly for them.

"Irene, let's exchange telephone numbers and e-mail addresses so we can keep in touch."

"I'd like that, Paul. Is it okay to call you? I mean, does your wife mind friends calling?"

"It's okay. I've already talked to her about the reunion and reestablishing contact with classmates."

Irene smiled and wrote down her information and exchanged it with Paul's. The night ended, and Paul walked Irene to her car. They stood by her white Porsche, with the full moon beautifying the warm evening. Silence! They looked at each other.

Finally, Irene broke the awkward silence. "I had a great evening, Paul. When we danced, I had flashbacks of our adolescent relationship and the feeling was both refreshing and scary. I loved it! I hope we keep in touch."

"I do, too. Those feelings flashed across my mind as well. I must ask you something that has been on my mind for years. Remember when you worked on the Jersey shore during the summers of high school and college? I tried to reach you all those years and left my telephone number, but you never returned my calls. That bothered me. I know it was a long time ago, but do you remember what happened?"

"Oh yes, I remember it well. I made a decision to stay away from you. I had gotten married to Jeremy and moved to Chicago. My parents were acting ugly during that time and I didn't want to involve you. I'll explain it further when we talk again."

"Okay, I just thought I'd ask."

"Paul, please stay in touch." Irene entered the car and pulled off into the darkness.

Chapter 28

Paul drove down the New Jersey Turnpike, headed home for D.C. The trip to the reunion brought him total satisfaction and Irene overwhelmed him. He replayed in his mind every discussion he had with Irene and looked forward to more contact with her.

Paul had concerns about how to carry himself when he arrived home. He felt trapped. If he appeared too happy, Terri might think something fishy went on at the reunion. If he acted neutral, Terri might think he was hiding something. And if he was subdued, Terri would want to know what was wrong with him. He was completely perplexed about what to do.

He also wanted to be extra careful about his demeanor because Crystal was home from school on a semester break. The last thing Paul wanted was to have her aware that he and Terri were having issues about another woman. He had a very delicate task ahead of him.

Paul pulled into the driveway and unloaded his clothes from the back of the car. As he was about to enter the house, Crystal greeted him with a big smile.

"Hi, Daddy." she said while planting a big kiss on his cheek. "Where ya been?"

"Hey, baby. I went home to Becton for my high school reunion."

"Oh, did you have fun?"

"Yes, plenty of fun. How's school?"

"Okay. I'm going to need my second-semester tuition in fifteen days, so can you or Mommy give me a check before I leave?"

"Just remind me, I'll give you the check. How long are you going to be home?"

"About two weeks."

"Where's Mommy?"

"I think she's in the basement. I'm going to Georgetown with my girlfriends, so I'll see you later."

"Be careful."

"Okay."

Paul went to the basement where Terri was folding clothes. "Hi, babe," he said as he smiled and kissed Terri on the cheek.

"Hi, honey. How was the reunion?"

"Oh, it was real nice. I got to see many classmates I haven't seen in years and, boy, some of them have aged so much. I guess they may feel the same way about me. You know . . ."

"Did you see Irene?"

Pause!

"Yes, I did, but why did you ask the question like that? You sound very defensive."

"Is Crystal upstairs?" Terri asked.

"No, she went out."

"I just asked, did you see Irene. Why would that question upset you?"

"It didn't upset me. But it was the way you asked. Look, everything was fine, I saw my classmates, had discussions with them, including Irene, and I'm home. Any questions?"

"I'm glad you had fun, and I'm glad you're home. I don't want to get into any discussions about Irene while Crystal is home from school. However, I want to make it perfectly clear that that situation may change after she's gone."

"I'm ready whenever you want to discuss Irene or the reunion. As I said before, I have absolutely nothing to hide."

Paul exited the washroom and went to his music room to relax. He played a CD by jazz pianist Red Garland, which made him think. After all, he had much to ponder.

Chapter 29

"Hi Paul, this is Irene. Are you busy?

No, how are you doing?

"Fine. I didn't know what time to contact you."

"During the day is the best time. Terri works during the day so any time before 6:00 p.m. is fine. Not that I'm hiding anything from her but the conversation will flow better."

"If you say so. I don't want to get you into any trouble."

"Thanks for being so considerate. How often do you visit Becton?"

Irene hesitated for a moment and finally spoke, choosing her words carefully. "Not very often, I'm afraid. My marriage to Jeremy was on the rocks so I sought companionship elsewhere. I became involved with an African-American man, and we parented our daughter. I took the change in my life in stride but wondered what my family would think about the situation. As it turned out, I had a right to be concerned because my parents rejected my daughter. I tried for the next fifteen years to gain my parents' acceptance of my daughter, but failed. Several years later, I tried to get them to accept Pamela's twin sons, but that idea also failed."

"That's really sad."

"Yeah, I know. I only went home when absolutely necessary, since it required leaving Pamela and her sons at home, an indescribably painful experience for me and my family. Consequently, I went home every five years and for funerals of certain relatives. And just imagine, I felt guilty when I had to answer your question because I haven't visited Becton lately. On the surface, it might be interpreted as suggesting my hometown had stopped mattering to me. Life can't get more convoluted than that. You have no idea of the pain we've suffered, especially on holidays. The pain of not being allowed to enter my parents' home with your most precious loved ones is beyond words. The damage done to Pamela by not being accepted by her grandparents (and Tommy and Teddy by their great-grandparents) was huge."

Paul inhaled deeply. "I don't see how you've been able to manage that scenario. I would have been livid."

"I had to show strength for my family; I couldn't show any weaknesses. My parents wanted no one to know their daughter had mothered a bi-racial child. They never saw Pamela or her kids. My aunts and uncles thought my parents' racism was sad and ridiculous, so they sneaked trips to Chicago to see them, never telling my parents. The pressure was enormous – even sick! So I cut all ties with my past, including former classmates, and started inching farther and farther west." Irene's voice began to crack and Paul heard faint sniffles over the phone.

"Look, we don't have to talk about this now. I feel the hurt in your voice and I don't want you to relive this tragedy."

"Hell, I relive it every day. It's good for me to talk about it because it's been cooped up inside me for so many years."

"Okay, Irene, go ahead."

"Pamela and I, and my grandsons, have spent many Thanksgivings with dear friends who happen to be black. We also spent holidays with good friends who are white. Both groups of friends are my 'real' family."

They ended the conversation two hours later. Paul became concerned with the content of Irene's discussion because she became very emotional. He called her later that day.

"Hi, Irene, it's me again. Are you all right?"

"Not really. I felt shaken after talking to you today. I've already told you more about myself than my relatives and even some friends know. You know, I want to write a book about my life, but maybe I'm not ready to write it. Or maybe the Fates sent you to me to serve as a kind of Boot Camp to prepare me emotionally to dredge up and sort out the grim details so as to be able to find the strength to speak cogently about discrimination, as I know it. I trust you and your intelligence, your insight, wisdom, and sensitivity, and sense of humor. All that feels very good, but I also feel scared."

"What are you afraid of?" he asked.

"Most likely I am fearful of being judged and disrespected. I've spoken to you about things I hadn't even thought about for a very long time. That's hard. And sometimes when we talk I feel as if you were actually helping me to connect with myself squarely. That's also very frightening."

"I don't know what to say. I'm astonished to know that you've been going through all this for so long, especially dealing with discrimination within your own family ranks. I'm speechless."

Irene continued. "I don't mean to bend your ear with my problems but our discussion opened up old wounds about racism that I've withheld for years. I'm having a terrible time processing my troubling feelings. It's a difficult time for me.

"In any event, I'm definitely grateful for you, Paul, and I promise not to become a burden to you. Why did you drop back into my life? We'll know some day."

"It hurt me to listen to you describe your fears and apprehensions. Nothing could have prepared me for this discussion."

"I have more, Paul. Do you want to hear it because I feel like letting this mess out of my system?"

Paul peeped at his watch to see how much time he had before Terri would come home from work. Good. It was only two o'clock.

"Yes, but only if it brings you some relief to talk about it," Paul said.

"Well, you remember my little sister Susan, don't you? Well she's the opposite of me. She doesn't like minorities. She hung around with a group whose ideals were one step below the infamous Skinheads. I'm concerned and confused about her racist attitudes.

"How can sisters be raised in the same household with totally divergent views about race? She never congratulated me on being a mother, grandmother, or great-grandmother. Oh, did I tell you that Tommy has a ten-month-old girl named Vanessa?"

"No, you didn't."

"My family in Becton has never seen my Chicago family. Would you believe that my sister is an administrator in a school system that is eight-five-percent minority, and makes over $100,000 dollars annually, yet she has no respect for the children and their parents? That really angers me!"

"Remember, you are seven years older than your sister. It could be that, while you were away at school, your father and sister were able to spend more time together, enabling him to impart his racist views."

Irene delayed her response for a few seconds. "Thank you for your provocative perspective. This possibility never crossed my mind. No one else in my life could have developed this viewpoint. We'll never know, but I think you may be right on target. When I listened to your words and absorbed the implication of what you were saying, my blood ran cold. The content of such father-daughter conversations sickens me."

"That's just my theory, so don't put too much stock in it."

"But I believe there's some truth in what you say. I also feel that you're able to have this expanded vision because you're black and that it escaped me because I am white. How essential it is and how supremely rich it would be for cross-cultural communication to be the 'rule' rather than the exception for everyone on this planet. We're here for such a short time. Life must be as full as we can help it. Life is really beautiful when we live it sensibly every day. Why are we so compatible after so many years?"

"Because in all the years we've known each other, Irene, we haven't changed. We like and respect each other the same as we did more than thirty years ago. Whatever adversities we've experienced in life did not change us."

"Well, enough of the pessimistic stuff. One of my proudest achievements as a single grandmother is raising my twin grandsons. I protect them fiercely and pour my heart and soul into their development. I'm so proud of how much they have matured and handled their school and family responsibilities. I've counseled them on the importance of diversity in our society so they won't develop racist viewpoints. I send them to the best schools, and I'm financing their college education to ensure that they are prepared educationally and emotionally to make a solid contribution to society."

"Did you dress them the same when they were younger?"

She laughed. "No. They always wanted to be different from each other. They're very independent, just like their grandmother. Tommy is the oldest, by five minutes. My most poignant moment is watching Tommy and Vanessa interact, laughing and playing with each other. Oh, if only Pamela were alive to witness the interaction. She would be proud, too."

"Do you have photographs of your life after high school and college?" Paul asked.

"Oh, yes, I have plenty. I'll send old photos of my college graduation, wedding, and abstracts from the 1960's, 1970's, and 1980's. I'll also send ones of my grandsons and great-granddaughter."

"Okay," Paul said, looking at his watch, "I've got to run a quick errand. We'll talk soon."

"Thanks again for your caring thoughts. Our friendship is very special to me."

Only four days had passed when Paul received an express package in the mail. It contained photos from Irene. He ripped open the package, turned on his CD to Clifford Brown's jazz music, and sat in his soft easy chair. Each photo of Irene brought back memories of their adolescent relationship. The photos were organized in chronological order, by year, which gave Paul a vivid sense of how Irene matured and became even more beautiful as a woman.

Paul couldn't wait to call Irene. "I really enjoyed reviewing the pictures, especially ones of the twins and your great-granddaughter. You looked like a perfect doll in your wedding dress. I'm glad you shared them with me."

"You know, Paul, every time I think of 'Paul Hodge,' I see you exactly as I knew you in high school. I instantly smile and recognize the familiar flutters. I now know two different persons named Paul and constantly and consciously try to sculpt them into one guy. Does that make sense?"

"Yeah, kinda, sort of."

"Okay, Paul, can you send me something about your life that I'm not familiar with?"

"I'll send photographs of when I attended college, served in the military in Vietnam, of my family, and a video of my retirement party. I'll send them today."

A few weeks passed when Paul received a call from an excited Irene. "The photographs were great; you have a lovely family. I was so impressed with the video. You've done so well. You've lived life so well. Awesome! But then again, not really. After all, you are Paul, and you lived your life just as he and only he would have."

"Why, thank you, thank you."

"As I watched the video, a sweet realization emerged and kept building. In the process of getting to know you these past few months, I had in fact been acquiring a new hero. You are a nifty person who fell into this realm for me, which is a very rare experience for anyone. Amazing! Further, the video also brought back to life for me – so vividly – many aspects of your personality that I *did* know well after all. What became clear through the words of your relatives and friends and watching you throughout the event was that you've been faithful to yourself throughout your entire life."

Paul smiled. "Thanks. Did you recognize anyone in the video? There were a few people there from Becton."

"No, I didn't see any familiar faces. In a very special way the video connected me to the memory of the exuberance that is unique to Paul Hodge – who was so important and attractive to me a zillion years ago. Your unfailingly unassuming manner while being the CEO 'of everything that is' was precious to observe. Kiddo, you have one of the richest families and family experiences this planet will ever know! I would love for every one of our classmates to see a twenty-minute clip of the video. They'd be reminded of how important you were to them and the class and how much they liked you."

"I never thought of my life the way you explained it. I'm just living it naturally and did things to ensure that I got this far. Yes, my family is very supportive of me and I don't take that for granted. I'm very fortunate. I am also very fortunate to have you supporting me."

"Paul, you and I are supposed to laugh a lot more than we do, just as I do with my best friends and colleagues. Let me phrase that another way: I'd love us to make that happen the way it originally did for us! I frequently have this thought."

"I think we laugh, but often we're discussing serious topics, such as your job, racial discrimination in America, the untimely deaths of Pamela and Jeremy, raising your twin grandsons. Our laughs come naturally depending on the subject matter, but it's there. Maybe seeing each other in person will stimulate more laughs than we're experiencing by telephone. Ha, ha, ha."

"That was right on time, Paul."

CHAPTER 30

Paul and Irene became reacquainted through music as well. It was important to them in school – and it was important to them during their adult lives.

"Paul, remember when we participated in tryouts for All-State Chorus? You made it as a tenor and the school was so proud to have you represent them."

"Yeah, it was a great experience meeting singers from other schools and working on new songs to sing at Carnegie Hall. I was sad that you didn't make the final cuts. I didn't know any of the participants, and the practices made me very lonely. If you had gone, we would have had fun."

"Wow! I didn't know you felt that way about it. I finally discovered that side of you after all these years. That was very thoughtful of you!"

"Well, you know, as youngsters we kept many things to ourselves and this is one I never shared with you. Irene, do you still like music and the arts?"

"Absolutely."

"Well, I do, too. I still view music and the arts as important to enjoying the quality of life."

"Likewise. I sometimes wish I had played an instrument, or danced or something. I try to go to plays and musicals as much as possible."

"Maybe we'll talk the first part of next week."

"All right, I'll be thinking of you, Paul."

"And I will be thinking of you as well."

Paul hung up the phone, wondering where this relationship was headed. There were times when he demonstrated strength in controlling his feelings for Irene, and times, when they discussed nostalgic matters, where he weakened. He became concerned about his state of confusion.

The following week, Paul awoke from a long, hard sleep and realized that Terri had already left for work. The day was sunny and windy, but beautiful. Paul looked out the window as the colored leaves swirled down the streets, piling into every street nook and cranny available.

Paul sat in his favorite chair, listened to some invigorating music, and called Irene.

"Who's your favorite high school classmate?"

"Paul Hodge, of course," Irene said without hesitation.

"The music I'm playing made me think of you so I decided to call. I hope you don't mind."

Irene hesitated a moment. "Of course not! I'm always happy to hear from you. What is that you're playing? That sounds so good."

"It's one of my favorite jazz CDs, featuring John Coltrane. Can you hear it?"

"Yes, it sounds so relaxing."

"Do you like it?"

"Yes. What other artists do you have?"

"Ahmad Jamal, Sarah Vaughn, Gloria Lynne, and many more."

"Please send me a copy of the CD by Coltrane. That first song intrigues me. What's the title of that song?"

"'Say it Over and Over Again.'"

"That's so romantic. Please send a CD by one of the female singers, too."

Paul sent them the next day.

"I don't have much time, but I wanted you to know that the music you sent is so soothing, it keeps my driving frustrations in check, prepares me for my day at the office, and makes me think about you. Music is pretty valuable, wouldn't you say? I'll call you when I get home."

Paul beamed with joy. "Okay. Try to call about three. We'll have a little time to talk before Terri gets home."

The phone rang. Before Paul could say a word, Irene began, "Paul, which two songs on the Gloria Lynne CD do I enjoy listening to most?"

Paul responded, "'He Needs Me,' and 'Make the Man Love Me' would be two good guesses."

"Well, you're half right. Besides 'He Needs Me,' I like 'Greensleeves.' Why did you pick 'Make the Man Love Me?' Is that what you think I'm trying to do with you, make you love me?" Irene laughed.

"No, that's not the reason," Paul responded, chuckling.

They were kids again, enjoying life to the fullest and taking advantage of their renewed feelings towards each other.

"A little bit of nostalgia, Irene. There were two black singers in the 1950's and 1960's that, except for racism, could have been just as good as Frank Sinatra, but they never got a chance to perform in white clubs or in movies . . . Billy Eckstine and Johnny Hartman. They were great! Even Sinatra said Hartman was the greatest singer he had ever heard.

"White movie directors in the 1950's offered Eckstine, who was very handsome and whom many white women dreamed of loving, subservient parts in movies as butlers and bellhops, but he flatly refused. He also refused to perform with his band in front of segregated audiences."

"Now that's an interesting piece of trivia. I never heard of the singers you mentioned. Do you have any CDs by them?"

"Yes, I'll send them tomorrow."

Irene called Paul upon listening to the CDs. "Thanks so much for the CDs. I fell in love with both of them. I want so much for my grandsons to hear the CDs to expose them to different types of music. I hope the generation gap hasn't widened so far that the CDs won't be as interesting to them as they are to both of us."

Chapter 31

"Paul, I'm coming to D.C. to attend a play at the Kennedy Center. I have some friends in the D.C. area and they bought tickets for me. I thought, if maybe you have some time, we could get together while I'm there."

"Absolutely. Just call me. Is there anything special you'd like to see in D.C.?" Paul asked.

"Well, I'd like a car tour of Paul Hodge's D.C. and why he loves it so much – one that would historically trace where you've lived, worked, played basketball . . . . I'd like to see passing glimpses of the universities – American, Howard, Georgetown, and George Washington – and the areas of D.C. where people live, prosper, and suffer outside the perimeter of Capitol Hill – how the city hangs together, but all through your eyes."

"We can do all those things. It should be very interesting," Paul responded.

"It would be lovely to walk and talk with you in the vicinity of the Lincoln Memorial. The Hirshhorn Museum and Sculpture Garden, a favorite of mine, is the only 'must' museum stop. Other desirable stops would be the National Gallery of Art and the Baltimore Harbor. And very definitely, allowing for spontaneity as we become reacquainted in person."

For the first time, Paul became concerned about Irene's somewhat cavalier attitude toward spending time with him. She never asked if she was interfering with his marriage or if her plans would place an added burden on him, even though Paul agreed to accommodate her. Paul just assumed that Irene expected him to deal with Terri and to find time to be with her. Although the predicament worried him, he was excited about seeing Irene again. He began working on a plan to make that happen.

* * *

The following week Paul e-mailed Irene, detailing his schedule for her visit. They talked later that day.

"Thanks so much for agreeing to take me to all the places I want to see. I'm so excited; I feel like a little kid going to my first circus!"

"I'm excited, too. I checked the weather forecast and it's supposed to be a beautiful week."

Paul went to work on softening up Terri. He wasn't going to be secretive about it; he wanted her to know of Irene's visit and his plans to show her around D.C.

"Terri, do you have a minute?"

A smiling Terri said, "Sure, what's up?"

"Do you remember our discussion about Irene?"

Terri, peering out the window and looking indifferent, responded, "How can I forget."

"Well, she's coming to D.C. tomorrow to visit friends and she's asked me to show her around. You don't mind, do you?"

Terri walked toward the kitchen, whirled and said, "I thought seeing Irene at the reunion was it. Now she's coming all the way to D.C. to see you again. What's going on here?"

"Nothing, and please don't twist things. She's coming here to see her friends and attend a play. She asked me to show her around because I've lived here for so many years and I would know the interesting sites. I'm just re-connecting with an old friend, that's all."

"Well, I'm going to be perfectly honest with you, Paul," Terri said, folding her arms. "Although I've never met her, I don't trust this woman.

As an unwritten rule, black women do not trust white women with their black men. I am a firm believer of that rule. So I don't know what this woman's scheme is."

"She doesn't have one."

"Oh, is that right?" Terri said, placing her hands on her hips. "There's only one take on this. She's up to something and maybe you're too naïve to know about these matters. But the sisters know what's happening, believe me. The sisters that I know wouldn't put up with this crap?"

"All I'm asking you to do is try to understand what's happening here. We've talked about this before. Irene's just a good friend and I want to show her around D.C. I'd do the same for your family and friends."

"We're not going to agree on this, so let's cut the discussion," Terri said as she walked to the bedroom.

Paul said nothing and retired to the basement to watch television.

* * *

Paul picked up Irene at the airport in his vintage restored burgundy 1962 XKE Jaguar convertible. They wasted no time hugging and smiling at each other. He lowered the top on this lovely day to get closer to nature. The conversation during the ride to the restaurant was non-stop. They used Irene's trip to D.C. as an opportunity to see each other again – unfettered by classmates, distance, job responsibilities, and the racism of the 1960's.

As they sat down for lunch, they stared at each other, smiling as though each had won a $300 million lotto jackpot.

"You know, I picked this restaurant because of its elegance, the great food, and the good service. I want everything to be perfect for this visit because I consider you a very special friend," Paul said with a big grin.

"Well, your taste for restaurants is great. I adore the atmosphere of a beautiful dining hall filled with gorgeous chandeliers and carpet decorated with lavish designs, great wine, beautiful waterfront, and an excellent menu. What do you recommend?"

"The gumbo soup and fisherman's chowder are excellent. I recommend baked flounder stuffed with crabmeat, smothered with a wine sauce, or you might want to try their shrimp scampi – it's to die for. The entire menu is great, but those are my favorites." They both ordered the gumbo soup and shrimp scampi.

"Do you ever think back to those days when you had confrontations and fights with those jerks in high school when we were dating?" Irene asked.

"All the time. All the time. They shaped my life and opened my mind about racism in this country. Yeah, I certainly do think about those days. What about you?"

"Oh, most definitely. I know it's never too late to show one's appreciation, so I want to take this time to thank you for protecting me and standing up for our rights so many years ago. That's what I admired about you; the strength you exhibited even as a young man to take on important issues."

Paul smiled and said, "Thank you. I was just doing what comes natural, at least to me."

After lunch, Paul showed Irene the high points of D.C. that some tourists never see.

"So, how do you like D.C. so far?"

"It's such a beautiful city, with all the unique majestic buildings, beautiful gardens, cultural diversity, theaters, and the like. I can see why you love this city."

"Okay, we are now passing through historic Rock Creek Park, established in 1890, said to be a gem in our nation's capitol. It features large trees, wild animals, freshwater streams with fish, park benches, picnic areas, and places to play soccer and tennis, and horseback riding, and outstanding summer jazz concerts. I used to eat my lunch here because of its beauty, and it helped that my office was not far from here."

They stopped at a rest station. As Paul helped Irene out of the car, Irene reached for his hand and held it gently as they walked to a park bench near a stream.

"Look at the tiny fish in that clear water. Isn't that cute?" Irene said as she got closer to the stream.

"Mother nature at its best," Paul responded.

"And look at those squirrels, chasing each other up and down that tree. Do you think they're in love?" Irene asked as she placed her arms around Paul's waist and looked into Paul's eyes.

"They chase each other like they're in love. Let's ask them," Paul said with a smile.

His smile eventually turned serious. "We really don't know each other as adults. That's why getting together again after all these years is so special. Just what is your passion in life?"

Irene looked at Paul and said sternly, "My passion is dedicating myself in Chicago Public School to the underprivileged. Have you ever heard of Cabrini-Green housing projects in Chicago?"

"Yes, but I don't know much about them."

"Please stop me if I appear to be rambling or preaching, but you've hit on the reason why I feel I've been placed on this earth. Cabrini-Green, built in the early 1960's, was one of the largest housing projects ever in the United States. Notorious for crime and gangs, it houses predominately African-American residents who live well below the poverty level. The children from the projects are left behind, especially with respect to equal-education opportunities. Guess who my students are?"

"I think I'm getting the picture?"

"You betcha! I teach at Public School 110 in Ward 27 where the majority of those Cabrini-project kids attend. I love teaching those kids because they deserve attention just like others in the city. There are a lot of untapped resources in that Ward because those kids are expected to fail in life. I don't think that way. I worked with many of these students at critical stages of their lives and was able to save many of them from heading toward a life of destruction. I even helped several students earn academic scholarships to respected colleges and universities. Paul, do I sound like a braggart?"

"Don't be ridiculous. I asked a question and you're responding. I really admire your efforts. What's next?"

"I'm very concerned about high-school dropouts. So I'm working on an adult basic-education program for 1,600 high-school dropouts. I want to increase their opportunities for gainful employment and college placement."

"How do you fit all of this into your schedule?"

"Well, I didn't have any problems getting my work done but because of the long hours I was putting in, it eventually interfered with my married life. My marriage dissolved soon after. Jeremy passed away shortly after I filed for divorce."

"Oh, I'm sorry to hear that. You had a difficult choice."

"It wasn't difficult at all. I want to be there for those kids," Irene responded as she nodded with tightened lips. We've lived our lives – now it's time for the kids to have a chance to live theirs."

Paul smiled as he marveled at Irene's goals, ambitions, and accomplishments.

"I'm glad I asked because I wouldn't have known these things about you. It takes a special person to do what you do."

"Well, enough about me. What about you, Paul, what is your passion in life?"

"Getting up when I get ready, listening to my jazz music, researching certain jazz artists of the 1940's, 1950's, and 1960's, and . . ."

"Enough, enough already! Don't rub it in because you're retired. You know what I mean. What's your passion in life?"

"My passion is to help African-Americans, especially the youngsters, improve the quality of their lives and to share with them my experiences in life. Remember those times in Becton? Remember those fights and racial taunts we endured?"

"How can I forget them?"

"Experiencing those years in Becton, serving in Vietnam, participating in SNCC at Shaw University where I did my undergraduate work, and living in Washington, D.C. after receiving my master's degree gave me much to think about. I'd just like to do my part to give back to my community and change lives."

"Can you explain what SNCC is again? I know we talked about it long ago."

"SNCC is the Student Nonviolent Coordinating Committee. It's a long story, but, essentially, it was an organization that specialized in nonviolent strategies, originated at Shaw University to end segregation in public places."

"What's the difference between SNCC and the Black Panthers?"

"Oh, there were big differences. Both groups wanted to eliminate white oppression and improve the social and financial status of blacks, but they went about it differently. The Black Panthers were community-based minorities who believed in violence and implementing the motto, 'an eye for an eye, tooth for a tooth.' They armed themselves and fought the police and anyone who challenged them.

"College students basically made up the organization SNCC. They helped improve the social status of blacks by implementing successful sit-ins at lunch counters in the South in the 1960's and 1970's.

"I want to mentor black kids – twelve through seventeen – before their minds are made up about life. I also want to get involved politically with various action groups to influence change, and work on political campaigns. Hell, I'm even active in my community as vice president of the civic association. I just want to do good things with my retirement years."

"That's great, Paul. Your goals are consistent with your personality – you've always wanted to help people. It is interesting to know that your goals are similar to mine. What about your daughter? You haven't said much about her."

"Well, she's just about on her own now. She's a sophomore at Georgetown University. Crystal is an independent-thinking young lady. I get a little jealous because she doesn't depend on me as much as she did when she was younger."

"Is she dating?"

"Yeah, but she doesn't bring him around me. She knows how critical I am, especially since she's Daddy's little girl. She's a beautiful kid, never gave Terri or me any trouble, and is serious about school. That's a blessing in today's society."

"I try real hard to understand the kids of today. I think I'm making substantial progress, but I'm glad we came along when we did."

"Hallelujah!" Paul shouted.

Irene walked a few steps away, looking down at the squirrels and occasional birds scampering from limb to limb. She whirled around and asked, "Why did you come back into my life? There must be a reason."

Paul's raised his eyebrows. "I missed seeing and talking with you all these years. The best years of our lives have passed and I guess I'm trying to make up for lost time. Another reason is that the racism of the 1960's would not allow us to have a comfortable relationship. At least now we can enjoy a beautiful day in the park without someone shouting racial epithets at us or the police shadowing our every move. It's different now, but the racism is still there.

"You know, I don't know of another person as warm and caring as you despite your numerous family issues. You've shared with me your innermost secrets about you and your family, you care for and help others less fortunate, and restoring our friendship has helped fill a large gap I anticipated with my retirement," Paul said.

"Wow! Your response was so poignant. Now that things are different, is that an invitation to restore our relationship?"

"The same old Irene – direct and purposeful. You're forgetting the fact that I am happily married. Did you conveniently forget?"

Irene glared at Paul, tightened her lips, and raised her voice in response. "Well, you can't have it both ways. You say you missed me, but when I follow up on your statement, you retreat to the excuse of being married. Which one is it going to be – do you want me or not?"

"What do you mean by 'want me?'"

Irene turned away from Paul for a second, and then faced him. "Okay, let's change the subject because we're not getting anywhere." Irene said.

Silence!

Finally, Irene spoke. "I reflected on what our lives have been like, and I see a real eerie correlation. Both of us are helping people less fortunate than we, people with no hope in life, given up, few values, and children whose parents have thrown them to the wolves. I am happy we shared our interests because we wouldn't have known that this part of our lives mirrored each other."

Paul nodded. "Yeah, that is strange, but it gives me a comforting feeling. I wonder if the Becton air had anything to do with this commonality," Paul responded, laughing loudly.

A plane flew overhead on its way to Ronald Reagan National Airport, smothering sounds of birds playing and water flowing between the large boulders.

"I know it's getting late, Paul, and I want to get serious for a minute." Irene nestled close to Paul and gently placed her arms around his waist. "I don't want to waste this opportunity of being with you. When you take me to my hotel, will you stay and make love to me? Please, Paul?"

Paul stared at Irene, stunned. When he responded, he chose his words carefully. "This meeting is like old times. I like you a lot and enjoy being in your company, but I'm only interested in our most treasured friendship. I don't want to do anything to disturb that. No sex, Irene! Please, let's keep it that way. Terri is already suspicious of us and now I'm feeling rather guilty."

Irene took her arms from around his waist and stepped back. Paul realized that he had misled Irene by sending the romantic CDs and apparently she connected the love songs with their renewed acquaintance. Of course, the tranquil and beautiful atmosphere of Rock Creek Park on a spring day helped trigger Irene's romantic feelings toward him.

"I'm sorry for my boldness, but I had to know if you still wanted me, I mean, really wanted me."

"That's all right, there's nothing to feel sorry about. Thanks for having a good attitude about this."

"Well, what else can I do? You said Terri is suspicious about us. What did she say?"

"I'd rather not get into it. That's between me and Terri. I don't mean to be so abrupt, but please understand the sensitive nature of all of this."

"Oh, I understand. It means that I don't hit the jackpot in D.C. I'm just kidding, Paul," Irene said with a smirk.

They headed back to the car and eventually to Irene's hotel.

"Thanks for the tour. I'm looking forward to the tour tomorrow."

"It'll be exciting, like today." Paul promised.

* * *

Paul and Irene drove up the Baltimore-Washington Parkway, through Fort McHenry tunnel to the Baltimore Harbor.

"This place used to be a real eyesore. They renovated it back in 1975, and now it's a main tourist attraction."

Irene's head turned as though it were on a swivel device, taking everything in. "It is absolutely beautiful. We don't have anything like this in Chicago."

"Baltimore set the tone for the rest of the country by showing that dilapidated areas can be restored and used as a resource, especially areas on the harbor. It has increased tourism for the city and state. Do you want to go paddle boat riding?"

"Yes," Irene said, smiling from ear to ear. They stayed until they tired and headed back to D.C. to the National Gallery of Art.

"I'm very interested in art. I've studied sculpture on my own, but I really love Native-American Art. Most of my office is decorated with it."

Finally, Paul and Irene headed back to D.C. and topped off the trip by taking in a twilight night baseball game between the Washington Nationals and the Atlanta Braves.

"Thank you, Paul, for making sure I visited Baltimore and the other interesting places in D.C. I could stay another week or two because there's so much to see."

"I'm glad you liked it. I guess I better get you back to your hotel."

"Good night, Paul. See you tomorrow."

"Okay. I'll call you about the dinner reservations tomorrow."

Paul drove home, wondering if Terri would question him of his whereabouts. The time on his car clock read eleven o'clock and he knew Terri would be up. As he drove into the driveway, he saw a silhouette of Terri in the living room window. Paul walked in, closed the door, walked past the living room, and looked in. Terri stood there, facing him, with her arms crossed.

"Hi. How was your day?" he asked.

"Good, and yours?"

"Okay. I showed Irene around the city earlier and later I went over a friend's house to watch the baseball game."

"Got a big day tomorrow?"

"Tomorrow is Irene's last day. I'm just going to show her a few places early, and that's it."

"Is she enjoying herself?"

"She loves it here and says this is one of the most exciting cities she's ever been to."

"I bet." Terri said in a low, inaudible murmur.

"Huh?" Paul asked.

"Nothing."

* * *

Paul picked up Irene about eight o'clock for an evening dinner at Hogates where he had made reservations.

"I can't thank you enough, Paul, for a beautiful week. Not in my wildest dreams did I think life could be this great. You made it happen."

"You did, too. I'm just glad that we became re-acquainted after so many years." Paul raised a glass of blush Zinfandel wine, held it to Irene's glass and proposed a toast.

"Irene, hold fast to dreams, for if dreams die, life is a broken-winged bird that cannot fly. Thanks for coming back into my life. I wish you and your family all the best that life has to offer." They clinked glasses and sipped the wine.

"Paul, where did you get that poignant poem from?"

"I'd like to take credit for it, but it's an old poem by black poet, Langston Hughes. I love it because it says so much."

"Well, we can thank each other for coming back into each other's lives. We're blessed."

Paul and Irene stared into each other's eyes, realizing that this would be the last time they would be seeing each other for a while. They took their last night together seriously.

"I could kick myself for not trying over the years to reach you. I could have done it. Look at how much time we've lost," Irene said with a hurt look on her face.

"I'm as much to blame. I could have looked for you before now. And besides, you've had your hands full with family tragedies and raising your grandkids. Compared to you, I've had a relatively easy life. I've had support all these years, being married to Terri, while you've done it just about by yourself."

"Shuuuush," Irene said as she gently placed her forefinger over Paul's lips. "Let's go forward, not backwards." Then Irene nervously shifted positions in her seat and played with her napkin. There was a long silence until she finally asked, "How are we going to keep this thing going? What do we want from each other in this relationship?"

"I don't know."

"You don't *know*?" If my memory serves me correctly, you gave the same response over thirty years ago. Of course you weren't married then and now you have responsibilities. But we're adults now. Can you or can you not fit me into your life?"

"If there is one thing that still makes me nervous, it is your direct and abrupt questions. Maybe I can, but right now I can't answer definitely. But now *I'm* going to be abrupt. I can't meet your sexual desires because of my commitment to Terri. Hell, we don't need to be intimate to have a respected relationship. For me, just getting back in touch with you is a miracle."

Irene took a deep breath, placed both arms on the table, and hands underneath her chin. She nodded slowly. "Okay, I'm disappointed, but you win. We can have whatever type of relationship you choose. But remember, we're in the last quarter of our lives, so we'd better enjoy it."

* * *

Irene surveyed the restaurant and stared at the beautiful art on the walls and the lushly hung white-on-white drapes. A bright half moon surrounded by gleaming stars appeared out of one corner of the half-closed drapes.

A well-dressed black woman approached Irene's table as she waited for Paul to return from the men's room. The woman pulled up a chair to the table.

"Hi, is your name Irene?"

A surprised Irene answered, "Yes, and your name?"

"Oh, my name is Terri Bianca Rogers-Hodge, Paul's wife."

Irene's face flushed. Terri looked directly at Irene and awaited a response. There was an awkward silence as both ladies faced off.

Irene gathered herself and without missing a beat, said, extending her hand for a shake, "It's nice to meet you, Terri. I've heard a lot about you."

"Yeah, I've heard plenty about you, too. Where's Paul?"

"He went to the men's room."

"Oh, did you excite him?"

"Just what are you talking about?"

"Never mind."

Paul returned from the men's room, astonished at what he saw. "Terri, what are you doing here? What's going on?

"I just wanted to meet the lady who excites my husband so much that he hasn't been the same since he attended a high school reunion last year."

"I told you about Irene and that I was showing her around town."

"Yeah, but you conveniently omitted this dinner. You told me you were taking her around this afternoon, so what's up with this dinner?"

"Oh, I added it at the last minute because Irene had extra time. Her flight was delayed so we decided to fill in the time."

"You're a damn liar. You ought to be more careful about the information you leave on the computer. I saw your itinerary and this dinner was definitely included."

Facing Irene, Terri continued, "Look, I've been very patient with this entire matter. While I am generally not a jealous person, I cannot help but think that your trip here is far more than just a casual friendship with my husband. Just remember: Paul is a happily married man."

Paul didn't know what to do or what to say. He found himself in a predicament that was very, very embarrassing and it gave him an empty feeling.

Irene came to the rescue again. "I respect your marriage, and I wouldn't do anything to disturb it. This is an innocent trip and resulting dinner."

"Yeah, right. Do I look like some damn fool to you? Why do you white chicks like to fool around with the black guys? They got something you like better than the white guys?"

"You're lucky to have such a nice husband. He talks about you often and I can see that you are a model couple. I'll be heading back home in a few hours and out of your lives."

Paul nudged Terri by the elbow away from the table. "Can I speak to you a minute?" Terri gave Irene a final nasty stare and followed Paul.

"Let's not take this incident to the ground. I'm going to take Irene to the airport and I'll be home in about an hour. Okay?"

"Yeah, Yeah. I'm going. I'm going. I just wanted to say a few choice words to her. She's not going to come into my settled life style and disrespect it."

Terri flipped her red jacket over her shoulders and walked abruptly out of the restaurant.

* * *

"How did she know we were here?" an emotional Irene asked.

"I screwed up. She said she got the itinerary from the computer, which I forgot to erase. Damn! I think we're going to have to rethink our relationship. That was too close."

"I'm a woman so I know how we think and she's not playing. If she sees us again or thinks we're trying to see each other, she's going to do something violent. I can feel it!"

"Terri's not a violent person."

"I think she has it in her."

Paul and Irene exited the restaurant and headed to the airport. Paul parked in front of the American Airlines terminal.

Irene spoke. "Thanks so much for a wonderful four days. I will never forget your kindness and generosity in taking the time to show me 'your world' through your own eyes in the Washington, D.C. and Baltimore areas. No one else could have made it more educational, pleasurable, and exciting. It was nice meeting Terri, although I wish it could have been under better circumstances. I certainly hope my visit doesn't cause problems and I pray that we can still maintain our communication. It's so important to me because you've opened up a world unknown to me previously – preparing me emotionally and providing the strength to deal with my family racism head on."

Paul smiled and said, "I loved taking you around. I'm glad you enjoyed it. I'm going to miss you, but I know you have to get back to Chicago. I grinned from ear to ear when I picked you up at the airport. The minute I saw you, I had flashbacks from high school of you cartwheeling during one of your cheerleading stunts. Say, can you still do those cartwheels?"

"If I tried, I might have to go to the hospital and stay in D.C. longer than I had planned. Hmmmmm! That might not be a bad idea. Ha, ha, ha!"

The solemn moment finally arrived. They stared into each other's eyes for almost a full minute. Paul reached for Irene's hand and they embraced. They pulled away, looked at each other again, then Irene closed her eyes and awaited Paul's kiss. Paul pulled her close and placed a long and passionate kiss on her wet lips. Irene quivered for a few seconds. Paul stroked her back softly, and hummed in her ear, "Goodnight My Love."

"Wow, that song is still outta sight and timeless," Irene said.

Paul nodded.

"I'll call or e-mail you when I get home," Irene said.

"Okay. Have a safe flight."

As Irene exited the car, Paul stared at her until she disappeared into the airport crowd. As he drove away he had mixed feelings about what he told Irene.

"Damn, am I fooling myself by saying I didn't want to have sexual relations with her? Was that my last chance? Should I change my mind? Should I continue to be faithful to Terri? Will Irene continue to put pressure on me? How will I react the next time I see her?"

CHAPTER 32

Paul's phone rang mid-morning as he relaxed, reading the newspapers after a morning walk. "Hello?"

"Hi, it's me. Can you talk?"

"Yes. How are you?"

"Good. I had a bad dream last night. A friend living in Florida has been sick and she's been on my mind. I dreamed that she took a turn for the worse."

"Why don't you call her and find out how she is?"

"I think I will. Maybe I'll call later. You know we are so fortunate to have good health, to be able to enjoy life to the fullest. But we can't take health for granted. We could be well one day and down the next. That's why I enjoy your company. You never know when the good times are pulled from beneath you," Irene said.

"You are so right. That's why I exercise and eat sensibly."

* * *

A few months later Paul called Irene but could hardly understand what she was saying because of a terrible, repetitive cough.

"Are you all right?"

"No, let me call you back."

Paul waited all day for Irene's call, but it never came. He started to call her but didn't. She finally called the next day.

"I'm sorry about yesterday. I can't get rid of this cough; it developed yesterday. My flow of conversation will not be smooth so I won't talk long. I made an appointment with the doctor for tomorrow."

"Yes. Please get that checked out and call me. You never know what it could be."

Irene called Paul as soon as she heard about her condition. "The doctors told me I have advanced throat cancer! I'm awaiting a second and third opinion on my condition."

Paul was numb! Silence! "I'm so sorry, I'm so sorry." Then, silence! "Please say this is a dream. I just can't believe it. Please let me know if there is anything I can do. Call me soon."

Within two weeks she called Paul.

"I have some very bad news."

"What did the other doctors say?"

Pause.

"I'm, I'm history! I'm history! They gave me from six to nine months to live. Can you believe it? Tommy and Teddy won't have anyone to look out for them."

"Listen, baby, just focus on getting better and follow the doctor's orders. I'll be here for you," Paul said as his voice trembled.

"Thanks. You're so sweet! My father knows about my cancer, so it can be public knowledge now. We'll keep in touch with each other and – cough, cough, cough, cough, cough. Then silence! Cough, cough, cough, and cough. "Paul, I've got to go now, I'm feeling very bad." The receiver clicked.

"Hello, hello, are you there, Irene? Hello, hello. What's happening?" Paul asked in desperation. No response. He tried calling her number, but the line was busy. He tried several more times to call Irene, but the line remained busy. Finally, he called the operator. "Ma'am, can you tell me whether there is conversation on 312 661-4571?"

"Hold please while I check the line." She returned quickly. "No sir, it looks like the receiver is off the hook. There's nothing we can do."

"Thanks." He got up from his comfortable chair and paced the floor for hours until his legs ached. He sat down for five minutes then slowly rose to continue pacing the floor.

A few weeks passed and no word from Irene. Paul's appetite dropped off and he showed signs of weight loss. He hadn't had a full night of sleep in weeks.

The daily e-mails Irene sent, sometimes twice a day, stopped. Irene's calls did as well. He missed the communication dearly. "What am I going to do?" Paul started to call Irene anyway but stopped abruptly. It was one of the scariest moments in his life.

* * *

Paul got an idea. He knew how important her high school classmates were to her so he decided to send an e-mail to the ones she was closest to, telling them that she was very sick. He asked them to send her "get well" cards.

Paul's idea backfired, big time! Irene received a card from one of her classmates. She e-mailed Paul immediately.

"You were the only one of our classmates who knew of my condition. Never did you ask me if you could inform my classmates about a very personal medical condition of mine. Of course, by acting as you did you gave the impression that you had a special position in my life as well as authority to act on my behalf. This was simply a self-serving action on your part that was not based upon the truth of the situation.

"The fact that you did this without paying me any consideration is incredible, that it never entered your mind to ask me if you could do this or if I would like you to tell our classmates about my personal condition. You just grabbed and ran with this opportunity, to serve yourself, not me.

E-mail me the names of our classmates that you told. Sorry, Paul, but you slipped off my list of friends with a resounding thud. Your lack of sensitivity and thoughtful reasoning was awful, untenable.

I'll look forward to receiving the names today."

"Damn," a devastated Paul said. "What did I do wrong?" Irene's e-mail tore through his insides like Hurricane Katrina destroyed New Orleans. His eyes started to fill up with tears. He e-mailed a response.

"I honored your request not to tell anyone up to the point of when you said 'it can be public knowledge now.' You didn't say not to tell our Becton classmates or anyone else. My only purpose in informing them was to ask them to send you a get-well card to cheer you up. I was being me! Your e-mail seemed like it came from a perfect stranger.

"The most disappointing statement you made is that I slipped off your list of friends. I hope that changes because my actions were meant to ease your pain, not increase it. I don't think I can make it without you because of our long-time friendship. Please don't do this to me. I'm sorry! I'm sorry! I didn't realize you would react this way. I am enclosing names of those persons I sent e-mails to."

Paul did not receive a response. He sent a holiday greeting card and newspaper articles of things he thought she'd be interested in. Irene responded.

"The fact that you continue to write me is simply a ploy to get me back in the fold. It is purely a selfish action on your part without any regard for my health. The extent to which you are driven to be self-serving is horrible."

Paul responded:

"This is my bottom line. Your beliefs and actions of the past few months have hurt me. I've lost sleep about it. I haven't been eating properly and have lost weight. I've taken your illness into consideration, but I don't understand your accusations. We should be embracing each other for making it this far with our lives, not feuding. I don't believe our disagreement is worth dissolving a thirty-five-year-plus friendship, but that's your call. Your motives for ending our friendship are baseless, but I wish you well. If at any time you choose to reconsider continuation of our friendship, my door is always open. I will always love you."

Irene's e-mails and phone calls stopped!

CHAPTER 33

Three months passed. Paul needed to get away to ease his mind of his concerns about Irene. He went to Mobile, Alabama, to see his friend, Bo, who served with him in Vietnam. As Paul and Bo sat down for breakfast at the Cracker Barrel restaurant, Paul's cell phone rang. "Oh, this is Terri calling. Excuse me, Bo."

"Hi, Terri. How's everything?"

"Well . . . Paul, I have some bad news." Silence!

"What is it? What's wrong? Is Crystal all right?"

"Yes, yes. She's okay. It's about your friend Irene."

Paul braced himself and sat rigid in the booth. "What about her?"

Terri hesitated again, inhaled and exhaled slowly. "Irene passed away two days ago. Her grandson, Tommy, just called asking for you, but I told him you were out of town."

"What? Are you sure?" Paul dropped the phone on the floor, his body shaking with grief. He gathered himself after a few seconds and picked up the phone. "It can't be true! Why? Why Irene?" he murmured.

Terri continued, "Her grandson, Tommy, mentioned how Irene told him and Teddy all about you and they wanted to make certain you knew."

"Damn, I knew she was sick, but now she's dead. I can't believe this. I just can't . . . . okay, I'll call them now."

"Be careful."

Paul's body racked with pain as he flipped off the phone. Paul said nothing for a few minutes as he shook his head and stared at the table. Finally, Paul spoke.

"Bo, my heart is heavy. I just lost one of my very best friends in life to cancer. It's too long a story to get into but, man, what a woman."

"I'm sorry to hear that. Did you know her long?"

"Yes, we attended high school together."

"Man, you kept in touch with her all these years? That's amazing!"

"Well, it didn't quite happen that way. We lost touch with each other for over thirty years, got together at a high school reunion, and kept in contact from that point on. I'm going to miss her dearly. Excuse me for a minute."

Paul got up from the table and went outside to place a call to Irene's grandsons. "Hello, this is Mr. Hodge, who is this?"

"Hi Mr. Hodge, this is Teddy. I heard so much about you from Grandma," Teddy said as he sniffled.

"I'm very sad to hear about her passing. She was a great lady. We talked about you guys a lot and the one thing she wanted most in life is that you and Tommy get your college degrees. She worked hard to provide financial and spiritual support for you and Tommy. Have funeral arrangements been made?"

"Yes, the services will be held tomorrow at three o'clock in Chicago at Haley Chapel on W. 81st Street."

"Teddy, I'll be there."

Paul returned to the table. "Sorry, Bo, but I'm not able to eat now. Can I get a rain check? I've got to get on the phone to make plans to attend the funeral in Chicago tomorrow."

"Sure, Paul, no problem. I'm sorry to hear about your friend. We'll get together again."

* * *

Paul boarded the plane and sat in a window seat at 22A. The excitement of the day had tired his body and the relaxing ride caused him to doze off into a deep sleep. He began dreaming about Irene and a relationship that ended all too quickly. No more two-hour telephone calls reminiscing about high school years, discussions about former classmates or our hometown, daily e-mails, discussions about racism and our personal experiences with it or advice to Irene about issues of racism in her family, or discussions about her proudest passions – her twin grandsons – or post cards from her many travels.

A loud thud awakened Paul. A wispy-looking flight attendant said, "We are now in North Carolina. Please stay in your seats if you are not exiting the plane. We need a head count of the passengers going on to Chicago. We'll be leaving in forty minutes."

New passengers boarded and, within minutes, the plane was back in the air. The closer he got to Chicago, the more nervous he became.

Paul reflected on the way he would act upon seeing Irene's family, especially her father, Mr. Dudash, and sister, Susan. He wanted to be cordial but wasn't confident that it would show outwardly. The single most important issue in Irene's life was to have her bi-racial family loved and accepted by her father and sister. That's all she wanted.

Paul arrived at Haley Chapel. The nervousness and anxiety he had experienced on the plane now was running high. He made up his mind on one issue: he would act in a manner that would make Irene proud. "I owe it to her." Paul mumbled to himself.

In the small, neatly decorated chapel, Paul looked around to see if he knew anyone. No familiar faces. He signed the guest book and sat in the middle row, on the opposite side from where the family sat. A small, frail old man cried uncontrollably. A brown-haired woman seated beside the older man held his arm tightly and tried to comfort him. That must be Irene's father and sister, he thought.

Two young men sat behind Mr. Dudash and Susan, staring straight ahead. One was holding a cute baby girl. That must be Tommy and Teddy, and Vanessa, Irene's great-granddaughter, he thought.

The organ played "His Eye is on the Sparrow," a moving hymn appropriate for a funeral, but it had a more haunting affect on Paul. Tears flowed down his cheeks. His hands trembled. He shook his head in disbelief as he viewed Irene's body from a distance.

Paul walked slowly down the aisle, his legs shaking and a wrinkled handkerchief in his left hand. He sobbed as he got closer to the high-glossed cherry wood casket covered with beautiful flowers of all colors.

A nurse steadied Paul as he approached the casket. He stood trembling. Several people formed a line behind him, patiently waiting in turn to view the body.

Upon viewing the body, Paul turned to his left and greeted family members. He shook Mr. Dudash's hand, looked directly into his eyes, and said, "Mr. Dudash, Irene and I were high school classmates and were the closest of friends. She was a jewel and resembled a flower in eternal bloom. I know your daughter's gone, but please know that she made a giant contribution to society in many ways. She had a heart of gold and would do anything to help friends and total strangers, alike. She simply was the greatest!"

Mr. Dudash squinted through his thick bifocals, and made several perplexed faces as his body shook of old age. Susan's forehead wrinkled, and eyes widened. "Do we know you?" Susan asked.

"I don't know. I lived in Becton many years ago."

Susan didn't acknowledge Paul's response, and with a stern look on her face turned her head away.

Paul then went to the next row where two young boys sat. "Tommy and Teddy? he asked.

"Yes," the boys responded.

"Hi, my name is Paul Hodge. Your Grandma told me so much about you guys that I feel like I know you both.

He shook their hands and said, "Boys, please make your Grandma proud by completing your education, getting a great job, and living a good life. She was so proud of you guys and wanted so much for you to succeed in life. I know you won't let her down. If there is anything I can do to help out – anything – please call me." Paul handed Tommy two business cards, gave them a big hug, and proceeded back to his seat.

As the service began, more and more people filled the small chapel. It soon became standing room only; many people stood outside the chapel as well.

At the end of the service, a black middle-aged woman of medium build approached Paul. She wore a large black straw hat with a black-and-white polka dot band.

"Is your name Paul Hodge, by any chance?"

"Yes, it is."

"Hi, my name is Muriel Banks. I worked with Irene on many projects within the Chicago Public School system. She had mentioned you many times, so I just took a shot at asking if you were Paul Hodge. I figured you had to be Paul because I watched you grieve over her body during the service."

"Well, you guessed right. Yes, we were very close and I'm going to miss her. Are you going to the cemetery?"

"Yes, would you like a ride?"

"Yes, I would, thank you." Paul entered Ms. Banks' car and they drove off.

"The cemetery is about ten miles from here so it's going to be a slow procession," Ms. Banks said as she adjusted her seatbelt. "You know, the thing that stood out in my mind about Irene was her aggressive approach to life. She was like a pit bull when she introduced her ideas and tried to get funding for them. She wouldn't take 'no' for an answer."

"Oh, I knew that part of her very well. She was the same person in high school. She was a dedicated person, even at that young age. She was athletic, personable, smart, aggressive, compassionate, and definitely an achiever."

"We're slowing up. This looks like the cemetery, to our right. You guys went back as far as high school? I think that's amazing!" Ms. Banks said.

As the long procession line came to a stop, Ms. Banks and Paul exited the car. The pallbearers lined up and took Irene to her final resting place. After the service, the family picked flowers and left the immediate area. Paul picked one rose off the casket and said a prayer. Then in a low voice, audible only to himself, Paul kneeled and said a final goodbye to his long-time friend, Irene.

"Thanks for re-entering my life. It was a short but enjoyable year, and one I never will forget. You meant the world to me. Thank God for the reunion, which built the bridge that enabled us to cross and connect again. Thanks for injecting excitement and joy into my retirement years. Thanks for the long, informative telephone conversations; thanks for the daily e-mails which kept me company, and thanks, Irene, for caring for inner-city black kids and about their education. While others stood on the sidelines, you got involved. You were a fighter, a battler, and called things as you saw them without mincing words. Every time I play the Gloria Lynne CD, I'll think of you because the songs on it are my most poignant memories of you. Our reunion was our time – another bond. Irene, as you always used to say, 'Onward!'"

Paul wiped his eyes, stood up, and looked for Ms. Banks.

"Ms. Banks, I'm going to take a cab to the airport because I have some thinking I want to do. I really appreciated the ride, though."

"Are you sure? I can take you to the airport."

"I'm sure. Thanks so much. Let's keep in touch," Paul said while exchanging business cards with Ms. Banks.

Chapter 34

Paul walked through the cemetery gate and caught a cab to the airport.

"Where to?" the cab driver asked.

"O'Hare Airport, please."

"Someone close died?"

"Yes, very close."

"Oh, I'm sorry to hear that. What about the rest of your visit to Chicago? Was it nice?"

"No, it wasn't." Paul looked out window as the cab headed west on U.S. Interstate 90. "How long have you been driving a cab?"

"Over ten years now."

"Do you like it?"

"It pays the bills. I also meet interesting people, and we have great discussions. I've talked with state legislators, U.S. congressmen and senators, movie stars, top athletes, executives, doctors, lawyers, and many others. That's the nature of this business – we meet everyone."

"I bet the discussions are lively."

"Yes, they are. You know, I've delivered four babies in this very cab, right where you're sitting. Sometimes people wait until the last minute to call cabs to go to hospitals for delivery. Man, you talking about being nervous. When you have a little life in your hands, as well as the life of a mother whose body is exposed to the elements, you should be nervous or you're not human. Are you married?"

"Yes, thirty years. What about you?"

"It's been almost thirty years for me, too. Do you have children?"

"Yes, one girl in college."

"Me too, but mine is only in the eighth grade. Do you still love your wife like you did when you first got married?"

"Yes, I do. As we've gotten older, we've also become best friends. That combination has fortified and stabilized our marriage."

"That's great," the cab driver said. My marriage is also stable. We've had our ups and downs but it's all good."

He and Terri had their differences but believed they'd come together when it mattered. Irene really tested his marriage. Although Irene was gone, he didn't know what effect it had on Terri.

Paul checked his bags and the attendant handed him a boarding pass. He walked around the airport, just looking at people. Who are they? Where are they headed? What are their occupations? Are they married, and, if so, are they happily married? he wondered.

He entered the airplane and headed to his seat. Then he pulled out his cell phone and called Terri:

"How are you doing?"

"Hi, honey. I'm doing fine. How did it go?

"The chapel was packed and Irene looked like she was sleeping. But it also was so sad. I held up pretty much, but I am drained. Can you please pick me up at the airport? I'm on American flight 4429 and I should be in around three o'clock."

Okay, baby, love you."

As Paul sipped his coffee and looked out at the white clouds and blue sky, he could just as well have been in heaven. The tranquil scenery was so peaceful; he reflected on his wife. Where would he be without Terri? She had been so supportive and understanding over the years, but his relationship with Irene really tested her patience. His insistence on renewing contact with Irene could have broken up his marriage. Through it all, Terri stood up well to the tension. Was he selfish for wanting an innocent relationship with Irene while simultaneously preserving the vows he made to Terri? He had to do something to show his love and appreciation for her.

Paul leaned back and smiled ever so slightly at the thought of seeing Terri through new eyes. He dozed off, to sleep.

* * *

Paul headed to the luggage carrier to wait for his luggage, then entered a nearby florist store.

"May I help you?"

"Yes, I'm looking for something very special for a very special lady. What do you suggest?"

"These flowers are very popular," the store attendant said as she showed him a "Flowers-N-Frills Bouquet" and "Splendid Softness Bouquet" arrangement. "How do you like these?"

"They're all very nice, but those roses over there caught my eye. I'd like three dozen of the red, yellow, and white long-stemmed roses. Please enclose a card with the flowers."

"Oh, I guarantee she'll like these. That'll be $225, please.

Paul headed back to the luggage carrier and picked up his bags. He waited outside under the large American Airlines sign, and continued to look for Terri. Several ladies smiled at him. One opened her arms, and said, "Oh, you shouldn't have." Paul chuckled and continued looking for Terri.

After a few minutes, he spotted his brown Mercedes in the far outside lane. He quickly deposited his bags in the rear seat, held on tightly to the roses, and kissed Terri. Off they went. "Hi, beautiful," Paul said, grinning.

"Hi, handsome," Terri replied, sneaking a glimpse at the beautiful flower arrangement.

"When you get down the street pull over for a minute," Paul said.

Terri's eyes switched between looking at Paul and the road. She pulled over to the shoulder. Before she could fully stop, Paul reached over, grabbed her in a bear hug, and placed a long, juicy, and passionate kiss on her lips.

"Well," she said. "What was that all about?"

"Oh, just a reminder that I'm still the passionate guy you married. I bought these flowers because I love you and think you're the greatest wife a man could have. I am so lucky to have you."

Terri examined the flowers and the innovative arrangements as she showed her beautiful white teeth.

"When are you going away again because I'll be expecting flowers every time you return from your travels? What's going on?"

"I've been thinking about a lot of things and I just wanted to do something special for you. When we get home, I want to have a long and frank talk about a lot of things."

"Okay, whatever you say. Is it all right to head to the house now?" Terri asked with a smile.

"Yes."

A "For Sale" sign sat on a house not far from theirs.

"What's with the sign at the Hartwell's property?" Paul asked.

"I understand they're divorcing and selling the property."

"Naw, not Eddie and Edie. I thought they were the perfect couple."

"Well, obviously something went awry."

"Yeah, well, it's their business. I hope they'll have happy lives." The 'For Sale' sign could very well have been in front of his house if Terri had really tired of his relationship with Irene.

After taking a quick shower, Paul hollered upstairs, "Terri?" No response. "Terri?" No response.

When he entered the bedroom, he found Terri sound asleep. "Good. Now he could calm himself and organize his thoughts."

Paul went to the basement and turned on the CD player. He searched through a list of CDs and selected one of his favorites, of John Coltrane and singer Johnny Hartman. If there ever was a CD that could ease his mind, it was this one. He cued up his favorite song, "You Are Too Beautiful," hit the start button, sat back in his large comfortable chair, closed his eyes, and listened to the beautiful lyrics.

> "You are too beautiful, my dear, to be true,
> And I am a fool for beauty
> Fooled by a feeling that because I have found you,

I could have bound you too.
You are too beautiful for one man alone,
For one lucky fool to be with,
When there are other men with eyes of their own
To see with.
Love does not stand sharing, not if one cares,
Have you been comparing my every kiss with theirs?
If, on the other hand, I'm faithful to you
It's not through a sense of duty,
You are too beautiful, and I am a fool for beauty."

Paul tapped his fingers to the classic piano solo, by renowned pianist McCoy Tyner. His mood was building, and he became anxious to restate his love for Terri. But he wanted to hear more. The next song, "They Say That Falling in Love is Wonderful," elevated his romantic feelings and brought chills to his body.

"They say that falling in love is wonderful, so
Wonderful, so they say.
The thing that's known as romance is wonderful,
So wonderful, so they tell me.
I can't recall who said it. I know I never read it.
I only know they tell me that love is grand, and,
If there's a moon up above it's wonderful, wonderful,
In every way so they say."

Just as John Coltrane started his saxophone solo, Terri called down to him. "Paul, Paul. Where are you?"

Paul rose quickly from the couch. "I'm downstairs, dear. I'll be right up."

He turned off the CD, gathered his thoughts, and went upstairs. Terri sat on the couch, scanning *Essence* magazine.

"Honey, did you have a nice nap?" Paul asked.

"Yes, I did. I was tired. What do you want for dinner?"

"Oh no, baby, you're not doing any cooking tonight. We're going out to a nice five-star restaurant. But before we go, I want to discuss something with you. I want you to know that I still love you. I know the events of the past year caused a rift between us. I want to apologize for that. But truthfully, that relationship was only a platonic one. Nevertheless, I acted selfishly in the matter."

"Did you ever sleep with her?"

"Yes. We had a sexual relationship near the end of our high school days, and after I finished college. But that was long before you and I met."

"How many times did you sleep with her?"

"Now Terri, I'm not going into detail about it. It happened more than thirty-five years ago?" Why are you questioning me about it now?

"Because I want to know."

"Well, I didn't sleep with her since we renewed contact with each other. I love you and wouldn't do anything to compromise our marriage. We have too much going for us. Many people would love to have the relationship we have, and I'll do anything to keep it that way."

"I still love you, too, Paul, but I must admit I was concerned about how you acted when you rediscovered Irene. It was like nothing else mattered. Whether you realized it or not, you changed dramatically during that time. You made me feel lonesome and unwanted at times. We stopped going out, you stopped calling me at work, and you retreated to the basement and stayed on the computer. I wanted to confront you when this whole thing was in full gear but I tried to put myself in your shoes. That hesitation resulted in me giving you the benefit of the doubt. I have not exactly been happy during the past year."

"I want to be totally truthful, so I'm going to share one thing with you. Please don't hold it against me. Irene was an aggressive woman. That strength made her the person she was and enabled her to reach great heights in her professional life. It also pushed her unabashedly to ask me to have sex with her."

Terri, with twisted mouth and raised eyebrows jumped up from the couch and yelled loudly, "I knew it! I knew it! I knew it! She didn't fool me." Terri sat back down.

"I told Irene that I had no interest in having sex with her. I just couldn't do that to you." Paul scooted over close to Terri on the couch and placed his arms around her. Terri leaned her head on his shoulders and they just sat there for a moment. She raised her head, looked at Paul, and moved closer. Paul responded with a long, passionate kiss that excited both of them. They caressed and groped each other. Terri tried to remove his shirt.

"Hold it. Hold it, Terri. Not now, we're going out to dinner first to celebrate a renewed commitment. Let's go to Keasby's. My mouth is watering for some fisherman chowder soup and shrimp scampi. How about it?"

"Okay, let's go and have that dinner. But after dinner, we're going to come back home and I'm going to rock your world. Let's phone the neighbors and tell them to close their ears."

Chapter 35

A year had passed since Irene's death. Paul pulled out the funeral program and reviewed an attachment which detailed Irene's accomplishments. He had never read it in its entirety. He was astounded when he read, out loud:

"Irene initiated the Golden Teachers program, which supported newly hired Chicago Public School teachers by hosting teacher orientation. She coordinated mentoring for first-year new teachers, provided targeted workshops on content and the function of a teacher, and managed school and system-wide efforts to bring new teachers into the system.

"She was instrumental in the development of the new Substitute Teacher Training Information, provided to substitute teachers in support of their efforts to provide quality instruction in the absence of the classroom teacher."

He glanced at the other, numerous accolades. Irene, even in death, continued to stun and surprise Paul.

Wouldn't it be nice to give Irene her proper place in society? he thought. Her work in the education and civil rights fields deserved a fitting reward. Let's see. Hmmmm. How about a tribute in her memory, like naming a school in her honor or starting a scholarship in her name, or both? Yes, that was it! Name a local school to honor her contributions to society, and initiate an annual scholarship to the student that most closely exemplifies her character, integrity, and drive.

The concept overtook Paul, and he immediately thought about a strategy. One name clicked in his mind – Muriel Banks. While Paul was not a Chicago resident and had no standing in the community, Ms. Banks did. He called her about his plan.

"How are you? I can't believe it's been almost a year since I last saw you."

"Hi Paul. It's good to hear your voice."

"I'm calling you because I've been thinking about Irene. I believe she deserves special recognition for her achievements, and I have a plan to honor her."

"I'm listening, Paul."

"I want to spearhead a comprehensive campaign by gathering the support of Chicago elected officials, Chicago education officials, grass-roots citizens, and volunteers. The result of gaining these supporters would be a request to consider naming or renaming, posthumously, a school in Irene's name. I don't have standing in the Chicago community, but you do. It can be your brainchild. What do you think?"

"I think it's a great idea. But it will require a lot of work. I'm willing to put forth the concept and see what happens."

"Oh, thanks. Meanwhile, I went on the Internet and studied the qualifications for naming or renaming schools in Chicago's public system and concluded that Irene easily meets the criteria. The policy manual states the two most important criteria: 'persons proposed for the school name must have been deceased for at least six months, and should have made significant contributions to society.'"

"Okay, that's good to know. I understand the power for getting a school named or renamed lies with the Local School Council and the Chicago Board of Education, with the board making the final decision. The LSC solicits the participation of the area instruction officer of the region in which the school is located. So we'll have to work on those people. I have a network of people that would support the request. How do we get started?"

"I'm going to fax to you a synopsis of Irene's accomplishments, the significance of her achievements, and the reasons why she should be honored posthumously. Please Xerox 3,000 copies and pass this information to the board, LSC, Chief Education Officer, the Mayor, grass-roots citizens and individuals, and to your personal contacts."

"Okay, Paul, I'm taking notes. What next?"

"After we distribute the information, I would like you to pick the alderman and board member you think most likely would support the request. You can contact these people by phone, introduce yourself, and describe the request for consideration you want passed. If these people support the idea, ask them to introduce it to the board and LSC and ask them to provide leadership to get it passed."

"Paul, this sounds like a great idea. Do you want to gather signatures in support of the request?"

"Yes. Anything legal we can do will be great. We don't want to be sorry later that we did not do everything within our power to make this proposal work. I believe we will be successful. Meanwhile, can you put me in touch with someone who can do a media blitz regarding Irene's successful work, especially her efforts with Cabrini-Green project kids?"

"Absolutely. Bernard Fox is an old friend who has numerous contacts with local radio talk-show hosts and television producers. I'll talk with him tomorrow about it and have him call you."

"I can't thank you enough for helping me with this effort. I'm so fortunate that you understand its importance. And for you to take time out of your busy schedule to help me is unbelievable. Thanks, again."

"I know you're on a mission, and I want to help. We're going to be successful with this effort. I feel it."

Chapter 36

"Have you talked with Irene's grandsons lately? You said you were going to check on them periodically," Terri added.

"No, I haven't. But funny you should ask about them because I got something else working. Sit down, and let me explain it."

Terri brushed her hair back and sat down. Paul sat next to her with his plan, diagrammed on a legal pad with yellow striped paper.

"It's about Irene again, Terri" Paul said, waiting for Terri's reaction.

"Go on." Terri said.

"You know, Irene died so suddenly, and I'm convinced that she has not been given her proper place in society. When I read the attachment to the funeral program, it was clear that she was an important member of Chicago's society. Her contributions to mankind were so outstanding that I decided to take the lead to get something done about it. You remember the lady I told you about at Irene's funeral, Muriel Banks from Chicago, right? She agrees and said she would help me. Our goal is to convince the board that Irene deserves to have a school named in her behalf. I developed a master plan on how to do it. What do you think so far?"

"Well, I'm not surprised that Irene is still on your mind, but this sounds like a worthy cause. Let me know how I can help."

Paul placed his arm around Terri and planted a kiss on her cheek. "Thanks for your understanding. It means a lot to me. It's going to be a lot of work because we're going on an all-out blitz, involving radio and television. We're going to try to solicit money to support our efforts."

"How is that going to work? You know money is tight these days."

"Yeah, I know, but I have that covered, too. I want to raise the awareness of Irene's achievements, mobilize board members, volunteers, and others, and attract favorable media attention, all of which will cost money. Therefore, I'm going to establish the Friends of Irene Dudash-Covington Fund to support our efforts and make this a legitimate cause. We will need approximately $25,000 to attract favorable media attention through short radio ads and TV spots; $10,000 to develop a Web site and advertise the mission of the Fund, and $5,000 for a fierce letter-writing campaign. The solicitations would ask for tax-deductible contributions, payable by check, money order, or credit card to pay for the ads. I'll establish an escrow account at a local bank to deposit contributions."

"Paul, I have a co-worker who can do the Web design. He's pretty sharp."

"That's what I'm talking about. Thanks, baby, for taking care of that part of the plan. Whatever you can help with I'll appreciate."

"Just let me know what you want me to do. If I have the time, I'll do it."

"Great."

* * *

Paul began the difficult task of contacting people who knew Irene, asking for their financial contributions to have her deeds honored officially. It was time-consuming, but Paul's memory of Irene fueled his efforts. He called a former high school classmate.

"Hi, this is Paul Hodge, of Hodge Consultants. I am contacting you about Irene Dudash-Covington."

"Yes, yes, it is tragic that she's no longer with us. She was special."

"My purpose in calling is that we are seeking contributions from as many of her friends as possible to get the word out about permanently honoring her. We're trying to get Public School 110, in Chicago, named in her behalf. In addition, we would like you to ask supporters to write letters to the board, LSC, city council, mayor, governor, state – elected officials, and relevant U.S. representatives to facilitate passage of the request. After that, please send me a file copy so I can keep track of the letters. Do you think you can do this in memory of Irene?"

"I'd be glad to."

Things were coming into place. Soon after, Bernard Fox called Paul.

"Muriel asked me to call you about promoting radio and TV ads in memory of a lady named Irene Dudash-Covington. What can I help you with?"

"Thanks for contacting me, Mr. Fox. We're attempting to get a school named in her behalf, and, later, initiating an annual scholarship in her name. I would like to have a lobbyist appear one week straight on three major radio talk shows and, preferably, during the drive-time morning rush hours, between six and nine o'clock. I would also like to have the same person make a brief appearance on three local TV channels during the dinner hours, between six and eight o'clock. I am waiting for contributions to pay for these ads, so I would say four months from now would be a good time to begin. I developed a synopsis of the rationale for these lobbying efforts, which I'll fax to you. I would like that information sent to various radio and TV stations preceding these appearances."

"Okay. This should not be difficult. We can talk about the cost of these efforts when I see you. Four months will give me plenty of time to get the right persons lined up to make this happen. I'll call you when the decision is made and dates are confirmed."

* * *

During a quiet period, Paul thought how wonderful it was for Terri to offer her assistance to this major project. "What a turnaround in attitude. No! What an understanding wife and partner. How many wives out there would be that understanding, given what I've put her through? Not many!"

"Hey, baby. Thanks again for your help. It's going to be a tough waiting period. From the looks of their policies, it will be an elongated process, and probably very political. We've put our best effort forward and I'm proud of the support we've received."

"Excellent," Terri said.

"I know I've been so preoccupied with this project, and I appreciate your understanding in the matter. You've been so unique in dealing with all of this and I'm lucky to have a wife like you. So when all of this is over, let's go to the Bahamas on a long-weekend trip. Okay?"

"Absolutely."

They kissed, placed their arms around each other's waists, and walked toward the bedroom.

Paul rubbed Terri's back gently and Terri stroked his face lightly, her eyes closed tightly. Their love for each other blossomed again. It all came together that night because they had a renewed understanding of why they were husband and wife – they loved and supported each other.

"I want to make you happy," Paul said as he made love to Terri.

"Oh, honey, I am happy and I love you so much."

* * *

Paul contacted the coordinator for the residents of Cabrini-Green to make sure they passed out as many flyers as possible about their intent to honor Irene. Their calls to city officials would be crucial. He was able to contact many of Irene's colleagues, ex-college and high school classmates about the calls and letter-writing campaign to support Irene.

"My contacts made the calls and did the letter writing to key city officials," Muriel said.

"Good. I received a call today from some Native-Americans who wrote letters to key local elected officials and made calls. Things are looking up. Excuse me, Muriel, can I put you on hold for a minute?"

"Yes."

"Hello, this is Bernard."

"Hi, just a minute."

"That's Bernard on the other line. I'll talk with you later."

"Sure."

"Bernard, what's up?"

"Well, I suggest the radio and TV ads happen the week of May 19 through 23 because it is prior to Memorial Day and to the summer vacation period. I would like to expose the Friends of Irene Dudash-Covington Fund proposal to as many radio listeners and TV viewers as possible."

"Okay, whatever you say."

"I was very fortunate to be able to secure a lobbyist who knows the process and has access to the media. I am confident that he'll do a great job promoting Irene's contributions to society. The cost of his efforts and for the radio and TV spots will be $22,500."

"Good. That's within our budget."

A few weeks went by. Then Muriel Banks called with some wonderful news. "It was awesome! The lobbyist did a fantastic job, Paul. We'll have to thank Bernard for the lobbyist because he definitely put his mark on the ads and promoted it at the highest level. If the other ads are promoted similarly, we'll be successful."

"Okay, okay. Let's give the ads a few months to soak into the minds of the various major players and make follow-up calls shortly thereafter. Then we'll make an appointment with the board and LSC when they convene in the fall. We should try now to get on the board's fall agenda so we can be the first new business to be addressed in September. That's when you and your colleagues will ask the board and LSC jointly to consider the proposal formally."

"That's exactly right, Paul. I'll have two good people that are convincing presenters with me. I'm confident they'll make a good impression on the board. I'm so excited about the prospects of making this happen for Irene. You've worked so hard to get this done and I'll work with you every step of the way to see it through. I'll call you in a few months with any updates. Bye."

"Bye, Muriel."

Paul could hardly wait to tell Terri.

"Hey, baby, Muriel pulled it off! We're about one step from holding hearings with the board and LSC and getting this plane off the ground. Isn't that great news?"

"Yes, by all means. This project is beginning to look like a beautiful mosaic of people from all walks of life, getting together for a common and human cause: to celebrate and honor the life of Irene Dudash-Covington. This definitely is a worthy and decent cause. The board will see it that way, too.

"Incidentally, how's the scholarship planning coming along?" Terri asked.

"Well, I'm naming it the Irene Dudash-Covington Scholarship Memorial Award. The criteria would be a fair and open competitive process. Two annual awards to one African-American boy or girl, and to one non-African-American boy or girl – the final selections must be a boy and a girl – within Ward 27, who are held in high esteem within their school community and who most exemplify the character, leadership, and integrity of Irene Dudash-Covington. One grade point average can be 2.5, but the student must possess good potential to improve academically; the other grade point average must be a 3.00. The recipients must have demonstrated volunteer work in their community. I'm looking at awarding $5,000 for each award."

"Who's going to make the selection of the scholarships?"

"I am," Paul said, confidently. "After all, I knew her better than anyone, and the qualities she possessed. I know it was a long time ago, but she didn't change over the years."

A few months passed by; Paul received another call from Muriel.

"Good news. I made contact with the board and LSC, and we're on their agenda for September third at nine o'clock in the morning. The guidelines are pretty straight-forward. I'll present the proposal, but two people will be with me to add all the supportive measures needed. Meanwhile, I'll be sending letters asking the support of the superintendent, the board, and all elected officials. We're set – and confident!"

"Great! Have a good summer, and we'll speak again before September third. I'll fly to Chicago on the second and probably stay at the Grand Hilton on Porter Street. I'll contact you upon arrival."

CHAPTER 37

The summer passed by fast. Although it still was hot in Washington, D.C., it had started cooling off in Chicago. The kids were back in school. The picnics and outdoor recreation and fun were behind them. It was time for them to buckle down and get serious again.

Paul and Terri arrived in Chicago on September second, to relax and think about the upcoming hearing. They wanted to tour downtown Chicago, especially the famous Palmer House and the transportation Loop, but Irene's business was first. They wanted to be fresh, mentally and physically.

Muriel called Paul at the hotel. "Everything is set. I'll meet you and Terri at eight thirty in the morning in front of the board's building. I'll introduce you to my two assistants and finalize my actions with the board."

"Okay, we'll see you then."

Paul, Terri, Muriel, and her assistants arrived in front of the building almost simultaneously. They were excited about the events that lay ahead.

"Hi, Muriel, this is my wife, Terri.

"I'm pleased to meet you, Terri. I've heard so much about you. Paul and Terri, please meet my two assistants, Ken Thomas and Alice Kendrick. They will support my proposal with their own testimony."

"Well, Paul, are there any final questions?" Muriel asked.

"No. You know as much as I know. Just present the facts, and let the chips fall where they may. We've done everything we could and it's in the hands of the board members now."

"Okay," Muriel said as she ushered her assistants, and Paul and Terri toward the hearing room.

The hearing room was large and had the ambience of a courtroom setting, only less formal. About seventy-five people sat in the long pews made of rich mahogany wood.

Paul and Terri were able to secure a seat up front where they could witness every detail of the hearing. Muriel, Ken, and Alice sat nearby, waiting for the opportunity to present their testimony.

The clock struck nine, and seven board members filed into the room, periodically peering out into the crowd. The mayor-appointed board consisted of seven members: two educators; two bankers; one consultant; one medical doctor, and one businessman. Two members of LSC were also present.

"This meeting will now come to order," Mr. Perkins, the Board President, bellowed out. "Is there any old business to conduct?" he asked.

"No," the secretary responded.

"Please identify the first item of new business," Mr. Perkins said.

The secretary said, in a firm and clear voice: "The first item on the agenda is a request from several presenters to rename Public School 110 in Ward 27 in their candidate's name. Ms. Banks will make the first presentation to have the school named The Irene Dudash-Covington School."

"Ms. Banks, please step forward and make your presentation." Mr. Perkins said.

"Good morning. I'm pleased today to speak before this prestigious board. The name Irene Dudash-Covington should be remembered in the City of Chicago's educational and social annals for many years to come. Irene contributed greatly to the betterment of society, community, and local schools. Irene dedicated her professional life to educational and social causes – to feminism, human rights, and equal opportunities – and particularly to supporting children at risk. Her many outstanding accomplishments, a copy of which I will leave with this board, are remarkable and must be honored in a unique way.

"My goal this morning is to make a convincing argument why Public School 110 should be renamed The Irene Dudash-Covington School. Renaming the school will have a positive effect in the community and give the public a sense of her contributions. When I complete my statement, I am confident that my request will be most difficult to deny.

"Picture an educator who: dedicated her years to Chicago's underprivileged students; designed, administered, and supervised an adult basic-education program for 1,600 high-school dropouts; volunteered to teach in Ward 27 where many of her students lived in the crime and violence-driven and nationally infamous Cabrini-Green projects; helped many of those students get high school diplomas and college scholarships to respectable schools and universities; initiated the Golden Teachers Program to mentor new teachers; developed the Substitute Teacher Training Information to improve substitute-teacher instruction; trained and supervised the award-winning Chicago Teacher Volunteer Program in support of public school teachers; reviewed and improved the process for evaluating test scores of Chicago students, and designed and managed the first voluntary elementary-school desegregation project in the country. Her accomplishments certainly do not end here.

"Her successful management of the largest Head Start program in Illinois is today a dynamic, complex organization with forty-five sites and 450 employees. It is modeled by other states.

"She conducted administrative and fiscal reviews of Head Start programs on Indian reservations throughout the country.

"Irene made a positive impact at the national, regional, state, and local levels with respect to educational and social programs. Serving as a consultant, Irene reviewed numerous federal programs designed to improve delivery of health services for children, youth, and families in America; developed an evaluation model being used to assess the quality of elementary education in Chicago public schools, and assisted public school officials develop innovative education programming for high school students.

"A dedicated grandmother, Irene raised twin boys from the tender age of ten in the midst of her outstanding accomplishments. And finally, ladies and gentlemen, Irene found time in her very busy schedule to assist President Barack Obama, then a community organizer, with community organizing throughout the communities of the City of Chicago.

"It is difficult to comprehend how one person could accomplish so much and touch so many lives. We believe it occurred because of her outstanding leadership qualities, her compassion for the human being, her unequaled character, integrity, and vision.

"Ladies and gentlemen, thank you for allowing me to present some of the accomplishments of this outstanding candidate. I trust you believe, as we do, that she should be honored by renaming Public School 110, The Irene Dudash-Covington School. My two colleagues have a few additional comments," Muriel said as she dried her eyes, concluded her testimony, and exited the podium.

Silence!

Board members stared at Muriel as she left the podium and followed her to her seat as she sat down. They appeared mesmerized and stunned by the testimony.

Paul bowed his head and sniffled. As he dabbed his eyes with a handkerchief, Terri clutched his arm and leaned her head on his shoulders.

"We'll entertain the next presentation please," Mr. Perkins said.

"Good morning, ladies and gentlemen. My name is Ken Thomas. I just have a little to add about Ms. Dudash-Covington. I had the pleasure of meeting her at a Cabrini-Green rally last year, protesting the demolition of housing units and displacing many families. The one thing I want to get across to the board is that she was not afraid of challenges. She took on at-risk kids from Cabrini-Green projects that no one wanted to teach. Her teachings enabled many of them to graduate high school and have a chance at life. She even assisted a few to get into various colleges."

Alice Kendrick added final comments in support of Irene. "Ladies and gentlemen, thank you for this opportunity to say something about Irene. You know the old saying, 'you can't do it all?' Well, Irene came very close. What I want to leave with this board is that she cared about the plight of all people. But she was intensely concerned about the status of Native-Americans in this country. Irene wanted to help them, so she spent vacation time serving on federal-review panels and redirected federal funds to help the critical needs of Native-Americans.

"In summary, because of the aforementioned reasons, we strongly believe that Irene is an outstanding candidate for renaming Public School 110, The Irene Dudash-Covington School. Thank you."

Paul inhaled and released a pocket of air. He kissed Terri on the check and held her hand tightly. He hugged Muriel and Alice, and then shook Ken's hand. "Well, the decision is in their hands. We did our part, and our presentations were outstanding," Paul said. He patted each one on the back as they headed to their seats.

"We'll take a fifteen-minute break and hear presentations for the next candidate," Mr. Perkins said.

* * *

"How do you think we did?" Muriel asked.

"I think we did great, but I'm cautiously optimistic about the outcome. I think we need to keep up the pressure on elected officials by having local residents call and write letters to the board and superintendent in support of our case. We can't take anything for granted," Paul warned.

"Yes, I agree," Muriel said. "I'll push my people to get moving on the calls and letters. Meanwhile, I have to get back to my business. I'll call you as soon as I get word from the board about their decision."

Paul turned to Terri and asked, "Is there anything special you want to do for the rest of the day?"

"No, nothing in particular."

"Great," Paul said. "I'm going to stay at the board hearing to listen to the presentations for the other candidates. I've got to see what we're up against. You don't have to stay. I can put you in a cab and you can go back to the hotel if you want."

Terri shook her head and said, "No, I'm going to stay with you."

"All right, let's go back in and see how strong the competition is."

The board heard four more presentations throughout the day and Paul and Terri assessed their chances.

"Irene's credentials clearly are above three of the candidates, but this guy Bill Martin is a concern," Paul said.

"Yes, I agree."

"I understand that this guy, Martin, has strong political backing, which could be dangerous when mixed into the decision-making equation. This makes me uncomfortable because I have no way of gauging the magnitude of the political pressure exerted on the board."

Mr. Perkins ended the meeting. "Thank you for your attendance and the supportive presentations. As you may know, this governing board uses an exhausting process to make decisions about naming and renaming schools and facilities. We take our jobs very seriously. Our final decision will be made in concert with the superintendent of schools. Once we reach a decision, we will announce it at another public hearing and provide the rationale for our decision. This meeting is adjourned."

* * *

The next day Paul and Terri arrived back in Washington, D.C. Terri had to get back to work and Paul was relieved that he got the 600-pound gorilla off his back by playing a major behind-the-scenes role to help Irene's chances for selection.

Four months after the hearing, the name Bill Martin remained on Paul's mind. It continued to nag him. He remembered that Muriel was supposed to oversee the follow-up, support calls and faxes to key people. "I wonder if her people followed through." Paul said.

He called Muriel. "I'm concerned about that Martin candidate. The people that made presentations on his behalf dropped quite a few names of support from all walks of life, so we know he has the political backing and that concerns me. Did your people make those follow-up calls?"

"Yes, they did. I think that's all we can do for now."

"I guess you're right. I'm going to be a nervous wreck."

Muriel laughed. "Now, you're making me nervous. I don't know how Terri puts up with you in your current state of mind."

"Hell, Terri's even more nervous than me. She's hooked on this project, too," Paul said, laughing loudly.

"As the youngsters say, 'just chill', Muriel added."

"All right, Muriel, thanks for your assistance, and thanks for the laughter. I needed that."

Chapter 38

"Paul, Mr. Perkins called. They've made a decision," Muriel said.

"Was Irene selected?"

"Whoa, they don't operate like that. There will be a special administrative meeting, at which time their decision will be announced. They've set a date of April 30 at nine o'clock in the morning. I'm so excited!"

"This is what we've fought for, and I hope it paid off. Man, I can't wait to tell Terri."

"I called you a nervous wreck a while back, but you should see me now. I'm no good to myself."

"We'll all be this way until we know what the final decision is. Just hold on a few more weeks. I'm going to make airline and hotel reservations today."

* * *

"Hey, baby, it's all set."

"What are you talking about?" Terri asked.

"You know, the board's decision about Irene. It'll be next Wednesday at nine o'clock. They're holding a special administrative meeting to announce their selection."

"I know you're excited and I am, too."

"Okay, honey, I'll see you when you get home." As he hung up the phone, he thought about the numerous steps he took to get Irene's accomplishments publicized, including: mobilizing people through Muriel to support his efforts, lobbying elected officials, delivering media blitzes, organizing support from inner city residents, and soliciting support from her high school and college colleagues. "I'm proud of my efforts, all for Irene," Paul said softly as he nodded.

* * *

April 30th arrived in a flash. Paul and Muriel and her colleagues arrived at the large administration room. Photos of past board members lined the walls, while the colors of the City of Chicago flags, official State flag, and a large American flag smartly decorated the stage. The podium stood to the right of the stage, with a large seal of the State of Illinois placed in the middle.

The standing-only-room crowd packed the room before nine o'clock. The tenseness of this special hearing was high and the outcome anxiously anticipated.

Board members entered a hushed room, as Paul and his group clutched arms. Mr. Perkins stood up and made some preliminary comments.

"Good morning, ladies and gentlemen. This meeting will now come to order. This is a special hearing to select one person's name to replace Public School 110 in Ward 27. All candidates were outstanding citizens of this community.

"I want to preface our decision by saying – and I know I am speaking for all members of this board – that, unequivocally, this was the most difficult decision we've had to make in the last ten years. It was made even harder by the many, many calls we received from outside sources in support of their candidate.

"We weighed many factors – background, education, training, awards, and leadership skills – all of which the selectee met overwhelmingly. However, the selectee carved out other areas which were unequaled by other competitors. The selectee had a great impact on human-service projects within and outside of this community. The selectee was a problem solver, a motivator, and excelled in conceptualizing. The selectee was the only candidate that had experience serving as a liaison to national, regional, state, and local organizations and programs. Additionally, to an issue that is sensitive to this board, the selectee dedicated a career to help at-risk kids and to the voiceless and powerless people of color."

Paul listened intently to what Mr. Perkins was saying. His heart thumped faster and faster. He almost held a death grip on Muriel's hand.

There was only one person in the room who was familiar with all of Irene's accomplishments. Paul Hodge! The accolades of the selected, spoken of by Mr. Perkins, surely sounded familiar.

Mr. Perkins continued, "Ladies and gentlemen, we wish we could select more than one candidate because it would have made our decision easier. However, it is our job to make the tough decisions in accordance with our responsibilities.

"Therefore, without further delay, our decision is to replace the name of Public School 110, Ward 27 with the name: Irene Dudash-Covington, effective May 20th. At that time we will have a formal public ceremony honoring the selectee, posthumously. Congratulations to her family and supporters for a job well done."

Paul stood up, with both arms raised in the air with clenched fists. "Yes! Yes! Irene, we did it!" He bear hugged Terri and Muriel and thanked the presenters, Alice and Ken, again. There wasn't a dry eye among Irene's supporters.

Paul eased his way to a side office, closed the door, and locked it. He sat down, with his hands clenched on the top of the table. He needed some quiet time. After a few minutes of meditation, he spoke to Irene.

"Well, Irene, this time we really did it. We really did it. I don't know what you would say if you were alive, but I hope you approve of what we've been able to accomplish in your name. Chicago now has a school named after you that the community and its kids can be proud of for a long time. We're working on a scholarship in your name, available for students who demonstrate your leadership, vision, and intelligence.

"You left this earth without our resolving the disagreement. I have to carry that burden to my grave. But I hope you've found a way in your heart to forgive me for my innocent and well intended actions. Please trust me, I meant well.

"I remember, soon after we reconnected at the reunion, you posed a question to me: 'Why did you come back into my life – we'll find out some day.' Remember that? Well, this *is* the day. You came back into my life to help teach me about life. I learned so much from you in the short year of our reunion. I was able to impart my experience that helped you to see through issues which had bothered you for years. We were so supportive of each other, and good for each other.

"Oh, and your trip to D.C. was so special. We laughed the way we did in high school and had so much fun.

"What would our lives have been like if we hadn't had another bond with each other? I would say mine would not have been as fulfilling as it has been during the past year.

"And it was so special to read about your professional life and accomplishments over the past thirty years. You were a real 'drum major' for education by imparting your time and skills to help at-risk kids and people without a political voice. Aside from your other outstanding accomplishments, those stand out in my mind because you already were at the top, but you cared and were kind enough to reach down and help others less fortunate. So there you have my final thoughts, Irene."

Paul exited the room and walked toward Muriel and the group, still standing around, buzzing about the selection.

"Muriel, I'm heading home tomorrow. Again, I want to thank you so much for your assistance. I couldn't have pulled it off without you. Let's talk about whom to invite to the formal ceremony. I have some specific ideas," Paul said.

"Okay. It was great working with you for this very special cause. It's taken my breath because Irene was so special, and I wanted to do something for her as well."

"Alice and Ken, thanks for your support in assisting Muriel. You both were vital to our success. I hope to see you at the ceremony," Paul said.

Both Alice and Ken acknowledged Paul's thanks and departed.

CHAPTER 39

Paul returned to Washington, D.C. the next day and began thinking about the next phase of honoring Irene. He knew he had to involve Muriel again, with her playing a major role, so he contacted her with his thoughts.

"I've been thinking about whom to invite to Irene's ceremony. I want to invite everyone whose lives were touched by Irene, so the list will be long. I'm concerned about inadvertently omitting someone or some group that legitimately belongs there. My other concern is whether Irene's family would attend if invited. What do you think?"

"All you can do is give me your list, and I'll send out the invitations. We'll set up an RSVP process and that's it. My name will be on the invitation so no one will know that you're involved, anyway. Can you give me an idea of who is going to be on the list?" Muriel asked.

"Well, her family; city officials including the city council, mayor, and alderman for Ward 27; a U.S. House of Representatives member; business leaders; Irene's classmates from high school and college; principals; American Indians in Taos, New Mexico; several at-risk students from Cabrini-Green projects, and the Chicago Youth Program officials. Irene touched all of these people."

"Can you get me the addresses of those individuals you plan to invite?" Muriel asked.

"Yes, I'm working on that. I'll get you something by the end of the week. I'm going to contact Bernard Fox again and ask if he can get us TV coverage."

"That's a great idea. Okay, I'll be looking for those names and addresses. While I have you on the phone, have you thought about speakers for the ceremony?"

"No, but Mr. Perkins would be one. I thought about Irene's grandsons, and you, yes you, Muriel. Remember this whole thing is supposed to be your brainchild."

"Okay, but you must be a speaker as well. This is happening because of you. This is no time to be shy, so is it okay to put you on the list?"

"No, I don't want to be a speaker. I'm just going to observe."

"Okay, it's your call."

* * *

"Hey Bernard, this is Paul Hodge. How are you doing?"

"Good, Paul. Congratulations, I heard the board selected your candidate. Man, that's great and required a lot of work. She must have meant a lot to you."

"Yes, very much. Look, this is the last stage of honoring Irene and I would like to make it a blast. I'm thinking full TV coverage of the event for early and prime-time news. I want those who won't be attending the ceremony to get to know her contributions to society. I'd like this last favor, Bernard. Can you do it?"

"This is a very interesting project and deserves coverage. Yes, we'll do it." Bernard said.

"Thanks, Bernard. I really appreciate your understanding. If I can do anything to repay . . ."

"Look, please, you don't have to repay me for anything. This coverage is bread and butter for our TV station as well. So this is strictly business with a little special interest on my part. Consider it a done deal."

* * *

May 20th was a beautiful spring morning with blue skies and few clouds. People started arriving at the board building around eight thirty a.m. Several TV trucks, cameras and cameramen clogged the sidewalks, spilling over onto the perfectly manicured lawns in front of the building.

Activist Jesse Jackson would have been proud of the crowd makeup. It truly was a "rainbow coalition." The audience included whites, blacks, Hispanics, Native-Americans, children, senior citizens, elected officials, a congressman, colleagues, high school and college classmates, and other interested parties.

Paul and Terri arrived around eight forty-five. They sat in front and gazed at the crowd that quickly filled the seats. Paul looked for Irene's family and spotted them in the rear of the auditorium. He rose abruptly and walked toward the family.

Paul stood before the family and extended his hand to Mr. Dudash. "Hi, I met you at Irene's funeral. Paul Hodge is my name, born and raised in Becton. I'm glad you could make it."

"Hello, sir," Mr. Dudash said in a shaky, barely audible voice.

"Mr. Dudash, my wife and I are seated down front and there is space for you and your daughter if you would like to join us," Paul said with a smile.

Mr. Dudash looked at Susan and said, "Honey, ya wanna sit closer?"

"Yeah, I guess so, Susan said as she gently held her father's arm and guided him toward the aisle. Paul smiled and started walking down the aisle. Mr. Dudash and Susan followed closely behind.

"Terri, this is Irene's father and sister, Mr. Dudash, and Susan," Paul said.

"Hi," Susan said in a low barely audible voice.

"Congratulations on Irene's achievements," Terri said with a smile.

"Thanks," Susan said.

Paul looked to the back of the room and spotted Irene's grandsons. "Will you please excuse me?" Paul said. He walked to the back of the room and greeted the twins. "Hi, fellas. I'm glad you could make it. Your family is sitting down front with my wife and me. Why don't you join us?"

"Hi, Mr. Hodge," Tommy said. All right, we'll follow you.

Tommy and Teddy followed Paul but sat directly behind Mr. Dudash and Susan.

The ceremony began. The national anthem followed the presentation of colors. A board member, in a stern and loud voice said, "The Chicago Board of Education welcomes you to this important ceremony, honoring, posthumously, Ms. Irene Dudash-Covington." He asked a clergyman to lead the invocation.

Minutes later, Mr. Perkins approached the podium.

"Ladies and gentlemen. Thank you for attending this important event. We are here today to honor, posthumously, Ms. Irene Dudash-Covington, her accomplishments, and to rename Public School 110, in Ward 27, The Irene Dudash-Covington School."

There was a loud, long applause and some whistles. Paul got the chills.

"Ms. Dudash-Covington's accomplishments are truly outstanding. I've been very impressed with them. The board had a difficult decision in selecting Ms. Dudash-Covington, but in the end, her accomplishments and contributions to society could not be ignored.

"Just look around you and witness the people whose lives were touched by her presence. We have people from literally every walk of life, representing all races and economic ladders, which is a testament to her ability to galvanize people.

"I feel cheated! Yes, I said I feel cheated! Why? Because I didn't have a chance to meet this great woman, that's why. You are the fortunate ones because you had a chance to work and go to school with, be taught and supervised by, or be just a plain co-worker of Ms. Dudash-Covington. You've all felt her energy and compassion for life. Yes, you are the lucky ones.

"I want to bring up Ms. Muriel Banks who introduced Ms. Dudash-Covington and her outstanding accomplishments to the board during hearings. Ms. Banks, would you come forward, please?"

Muriel, dressed in a smart brown suit with a yellow-and-brown-striped silk scarf, walked to the podium and nodded to familiar faces in the crowd. "To the board, distinguished guests, and ladies and gentlemen. It is a pleasure to be here to honor Irene. I'd like to call her Irene if you don't mind because she was one of my closest friends. We hit it off immediately after we met. She was an outstanding leader of programs and people and loved life to the fullest. She had passion for people and was there for anyone who asked for her services. Naming Public School 110, The Irene Dudash-Covington School is an outstanding tribute to this community.

"Mr. Perkins, I know this isn't part of the program, but I must deviate a bit. I met this man at Irene's funeral. We had discussion and I realized how close he and Irene were. The main reason all of us are here this morning is because of him. He is the one who encouraged, no, demanded that I get involved and introduce Irene's accomplishments to the board. He has known her longer than anyone in this auditorium, except for her family. Paul, can you come up here, please?"

Paul was stunned! What's going on here? Paul thought. He hesitated.

Terri smiled and said, "Go ahead, Paul, go ahead."

Paul slowly got up and headed to the podium. He adjusted his lavender silk tie and buttoned his charcoal grey, pinstripe suit jacket as he walked up the stairs toward the podium. As he reached the final stair, Paul and Muriel hugged each other.

"Ladies and gentlemen, this is Paul Hodge," Muriel said. "Although he doesn't live in this community, Paul had a vision to honor Irene. Paul, all the way from Washington, D.C., is the one who galvanized our community to push the board to honor her. He trusted me to lead the charge and I am so glad I took on the challenge. It's been a truly humbling and spiritually rewarding experience. Paul, I know I caught you by surprise, but please say a few words," Muriel said as she stepped aside.

"Thanks, Muriel. Paul hesitated a few seconds while he gathered his thoughts. "If Irene were here, looking over this vast, diverse audience, she would sum it up in one word: 'Wow!'" The audience nodded.

"All Irene wanted in life was to help people and to make a difference. We all know she accomplished that goal. She fell short on some very personal goals, but never stopped trying. Irene loved her family and friends and fought fiercely to protect them. She was so very proud of her deceased daughter, Pamela, her twin grandsons, Tommy and Teddy, and her great-granddaughter, Vanessa. She shared with me that all four strengthened her life and eased some personal pain she was going through.

"I just want to say that I am so fortunate to have known Irene. I'm even more blessed that I bonded with her again at our high school class reunion after so many years of not seeing or hearing from her. It allowed me to know her as an adult and witness her growth from her adolescent years. She was an amazing person!

"This honor, which is being bestowed on her today, is very fitting. Through the Irene Dudash-Covington School, her memory will carry on. I've personally set up an academic scholarship of two awards, for two students that exemplify her leadership, work ethic, intelligence, and integrity. I will try to get Stanford University, her alma mater, to continue the scholarship after the first year.

"I would like for everyone to bow your heads for a moment of silence in remembrance of Irene."

Silence.

"Thank you, and special thanks to you, Muriel, for giving me this opportunity to say a few words about Irene."

Paul walked back to his seat to a round of applause. He kissed Terri and shook hands with Irene's family.

Muriel gave Mr. Perkins the microphone.

"Ladies and gentlemen, this now features the special portion of this ceremony. Would Irene's grandchildren, Tommy and Teddy, come up, please?"

The heads of Mr. Dudash and Susan snapped around to the movement behind them. Tommy and Teddy headed to the stage.

"Tommy and Teddy, I am proud to present this plaque to you both, honoring your grandmother, posthumously. It states: 'Presented to the family of Ms. Irene Dudash-Covington, for her outstanding thirty years of dedication and commitment to the Chicago Public School system. Her deeds merit renaming Public School 110, The Irene Dudash-Covington School.' Congratulations boys." Mr. Perkins handed Tommy the plaque.

Tommy and Teddy smiled and surveyed the crowd as Teddy pulled out a small piece of paper. "Thank you, ladies and gentlemen, and distinguished guests. We are proud to accept this honor on behalf of our family. Grandma made sure our lives went in the right direction. She taught us something every day and looked for good things in our upbringing. She raised us during the time when our mother was very sick. I think it was at that time we saw the strength and character she possessed. One of Grandma's goals was to make sure we graduated from college. We're almost there, and we will finish. We thank the board and the City of Chicago for honoring our grandmother, and special thanks to Mr. Hodge and Ms. Banks for making it happen."

Paul nodded. Tommy and Teddy walked back to their seats, never once looking at Mr. Dudash and Susan.

"This concludes the ceremony. All the best to the Dudash-Covington family," Mr. Perkins said.

Members of the audience congratulated Tommy and Teddy and Mr. Dudash and Susan in two different groups.

Paul looked at Terri. "I've got make a bold move – it may work and it may not. But I've got to try."

"What are you going to do?" Terri asked.

Paul walked over to Tommy and Teddy. "Tommy, why don't you and Teddy go over to your family and introduce yourselves? Your grandmother told me all about how they mistreated your mother and her, but this is a good time to try to mend family differences. Your grandmother and mother are gone now, so you guys are the only ones left to straighten out this mess. Your grandmother would be so proud of you guys if you took this daring step."

Tommy looked at Teddy and bowed his head. Staring at the ground, Tommy said, "I don't know, Mr. Hodge. They don't like us because we're bi-racial and they never invited us to their home. Grandma told us long ago how it hurt both her and mommy. I guess that's why she kept us away from them all our lives."

"Yeah," chimed in Teddy. "I'm not going."

"Look, you guys have all the reason in the world to be upset. I'd be, too. You guys soon will graduate from college and head out into the world to live your lives. You'll find that not everything is fair out there, including family matters."

Silence!

Paul made one last attempt. "Fellas, please try for your Mom and Grandma. You don't want little Vanessa to not know her family, do you?

Don't let this opportunity slip away because you don't know when you'll see them, again. Show them that you are educated young men who will overlook their years of prejudice towards your family. Just remember that you are all one family, regardless of your mixed race."

Tommy looked at Teddy and shrugged his shoulders. "Oh boy, this is gonna be hard. Do you want to do it Teddy?" Tommy asked.

Teddy fixed his gaze on Mr. Dudash and Susan for a few seconds. "Okay, let's do it for Mom, Grandma, and Vanessa," Teddy said as he tightened up his lips.

Tommy and Teddy walked casually over to Mr. Dudash and Susan and started talking.

Paul felt a chill run through his body as he witnessed Tommy and Teddy actually talking to their *other* family. "If only Irene were here to see the Dudash family making history. What a sight! What a sight!" Paul whispered to himself. He stood there for a moment and smiled as he went back to Terri.

Paul took Terri by the hand and walked out of the auditorium, never looking back. But of course, Irene would never be far from his thoughts.

Wow!

Edwards Brothers Inc.
Blue Ridge Summit, PA. USA
May 23, 2011